How To Achieve
Permanent
Motivation

E. B. Alexander

Dedication

To the ones who almost gave up.

To the ones who kept showing up.

This is for you—

Not because you never fell.

But because you chose to rise, more times than you sank.

Table of Contents

Acknowledgment

To every reader who picked up this book with even a flicker of hope, I thank you. Your silent courage, your questions, your hunger for change inspired me more than you know. You reminded me that love is not just something we receive, but something we give back through our work, our words, and our willingness to grow. This book was written with you in mind, and my deepest hope is that it helps you see your worth, find your strength, and carry your light into the world.

About the Author

The author of *How to Achieve Permanent Motivation* is a speaker, teacher, and creative entrepreneur with a passion for helping people unlock their inner strength. With a background in personal development, leadership, and spiritual growth, the author has spent years studying the deep roots of motivation, why it fades, why it matters, and how it can become lasting.

Known for a bold yet grounded voice, the author speaks directly to the heart of the reader, challenging shallow motivation and replacing it with purpose-driven clarity. Rather than relying on hype or hollow promises, their work is centered on truth, healing, and action.

This book is not theory. It's a reflection of personal experience, hard-won insight, and a desire to see others live from wholeness instead of hustle. Whether guiding individuals through mental shifts or coaching entrepreneurs through purpose-aligned decisions, the author's mission is clear: to help others rise without losing themselves in the process.

Permanent Motivation

You will not change because you are not worth it.

Do you believe the above statement? Most people have been conditioned to believe it and have bought that lie, lock, stock, and barrel. You believe your worth is in accomplishment and material things, not in your presence.

Your very being means nothing to you; it feels like a burden that must be numbed with external pleasures.

What you do to survive is not truly you, it is you enslaved. But you go on pretending it's you because you are not you. And if you were truly yourself, you would hate that version of you.

I know the statements above may not sound like traditional motivation, but let me be honest before we get to that. I was told this book should be softer, full of fluff and sugar-coated lines that gently pull the reader in. I was warned that strong language would backfire, that being direct would alienate people.

I was told I was assuming too much, assuming that readers don't believe they're worth it, and that it would offend them enough to put the book down.

But isn't that a shame?

We've grown so sensitive that people feel the need to speak to us like fragile pets rather than competent adults. So I decided: I stripped out what was meant to soothe the timid and kept what might awaken the strong. Because if your motivation can't survive honesty, it won't survive life.

"The principal rule of logic is to remain the principal. Never let the principles of others override your authority.
When fear becomes the principal, true principles fall. Be principal in your logic, and fear will never rule your principles."

— E. A.

***

"SOME SUBJECTS ARE REPEATED IN THIS BOOK TO DRIVE THEM HOME."

Lines are provided throughout the book to write down your thoughts.

_____
_____
_____
_____
_____
_____
_____
_____
_____
_____
_____
_____
_____
_____
_____
_____
_____
_____

Page Left Blank Intentionally

Introduction

The Missing Piece

There is a mental health crisis in the world, and while its causes are complex and varied, one factor often gets overlooked in our discussions of treatment and healing: the human need for meaning and purpose. It is not just the result of bad luck, poor habits, or chemical imbalances. At its core, it stems from a lack of life-giving motivation. And that is another way of saying there is a lack of God in the world.

Let me make this clear: this book has nothing to do with religion.

Doctors focus extensively on brain chemistry, trauma, genetics, and environmental factors, all crucial elements that require professional attention. But alongside these clinical realities, there exists a major crisis: the erosion of what gives life meaning.

I'm talking about a purpose that extends beyond the self, creativity that serves something larger than personal gain, presence that comes from knowing you belong somewhere and to someone, protection that comes from values worth defending, leadership that emerges when you recognize your responsibility to contribute, and the amazing strength that grows from understanding why you're here.

Purpose as Medicine

Purpose is a powerful force in the healing process, not a cure for illness, but a catalyst that strengthens your will to recover and grow beyond your current circumstances. It offers something meaningful to reach toward when pain, depression, or despair feels overwhelming.

Without a sense of purpose, healing becomes much more difficult because you lack the motivation to do the hard work that recovery requires. This isn't a judgment; it's simply how human psychology works. We need reasons to fight through difficulty, reasons to persist when everything feels hopeless, and reasons to believe that the effort is worth it.

Purpose provides that reason. It gives suffering context and direction. Instead of asking, *"Why is this happening to me?"* you begin asking, *"How can I use this experience to become who I'm meant to be?"* or *"What can I learn from this that will help me serve something greater than my immediate comfort?"*

This shift in perspective is crucial because true recovery isn't about returning to who you were before the crisis, trauma, or illness. It's about building a life that's genuinely worth living, one that has meaning, connection, and the kind of resilience that comes from knowing your struggles serve a larger purpose.

When you have something meaningful to live for, your body's natural healing mechanisms work more effectively. Your mind becomes more focused on solutions rather than problems. Your spirit finds strength you didn't know existed. This isn't magical thinking; it's the documented reality of how purpose affects both mental and physical health.

The darkness of despair, addiction, depression, or chronic illness thrives in the absence of meaning. But when you discover, or rediscover, your purpose for being here, your unique contribution to the world, the darkness loses its power over you.

Recovery becomes not just about surviving another day, but about building the life you were always meant to live. That vision of a meaningful future becomes the medicine that helps carry you through the healing process.

Mental health treatment requires professional care, medication when needed, therapy, and community support. But it also benefits from meaning, purpose, and connection to something transcendent, not as a replacement for clinical care, but as a complement to it.

When we ignore this dimension of human flourishing, we leave people with functioning brains but empty lives. Healing the mind while nourishing the spirit both matter in the journey toward wholeness.

The Soul's True Hunger

Every soul yearns to be more than what it has been conditioned to believe about its purpose. Notice I said *soul*, not *person* or *flesh*. The soul operates on a higher frequency than the flesh and cannot be satisfied by what satisfies the flesh.

The flesh finds its worth in worldly accomplishments, the title, the salary, the possessions that announce your status to others. But the soul finds itself through genuine human growth. This is the process by which people of depth connect with one another in pursuit of authentic love, meaningful life, and eternal peace.

It's a spiritual awakening that has nothing to do with shallow declarations of universal love, because true love requires focus and energy. Those who claim to love everyone actually love no one deeply enough to matter.

Human growth is the soul's desire to become illuminated once again, to remember what it knew before the world taught it to settle for less. This is why money alone never provides lasting motivation. Your soul recognizes the difference between working to contribute something meaningful and simply being charged rent to exist on the planet that was freely given to all of us.

We were never meant to pay for the privilege of being alive on Earth. Yet most of our energy goes toward earning the right to occupy space that belongs to no one and everyone at the same time. Working to create, serve, and grow feeds the soul. Working merely to afford existence starves it.

More people are awakening to this distinction. They are recognizing that their deepest dissatisfaction isn't about having too little money, but about spending their lives in service to a system that treats survival as a commodity rather than a birthright.

GOD

This short book is not another motivational hype session. It lays the foundation for something very few people discuss: cultivating *permanent* motivation.

You hear about motivation all the time, but it usually burns out within days. That's not motivation, that's a performance. That's survival mode dressed up as ambition. What the world teaches today isn't motivation; it's modern-day slavery with better marketing.

You're being told to chase dreams that were never yours, to fill your life with things that empty your soul. Greed, lust, materialism, and exhaustion, all repackaged as success. Meanwhile, you're left drowning in stress, mentally sick, and spiritually numb.

But permanent motivation is not about chasing anything. It's about returning to yourself. It's already in you. It lives inside the same body you've been told to hate, ignore, or push to the limit.

Your mind is a gift, not a tool for someone else's profit. Not a machine to be borrowed, manipulated, and burned out. But most people never consider how much their job and lifestyle use up their minds. They separate the mind and body as if one can be drained while the other keeps thriving.

Every time you drag your body to do something you hate, your mind is paying the price. You think you're tired because you worked hard. But what if you're tired because someone else has been using your mind to build a world you don't even believe in?

Work is admirable, and it's healthy. It gives structure, meaning, and sometimes even joy. The old folks in the South used to say it helps you sleep right at night, and they were right. There is something good about honest work.

But when work becomes the reason you live, when your identity gets wrapped up in the grind, you haven't found success. You've walked out of life and into death.

Permanent motivation starts with a decision. It's the decision to say: *"My life is worth more than what I've accepted."*

It sounds simple when you read it. But living it? That's another story. Choosing self-worth in a world that profits from your insecurity is one of the hardest things you'll ever do.

Most people don't even think about self-worth because they believe they are worthless. And isn't that embarrassing?

We've built entire industries on distraction, comparison, and overwork. We've made it easier to learn how to code artificial intelligence than it is to learn how to value ourselves. That should stop you in your tracks.

Because if you don't believe in your worth, your gifts won't matter. Your work won't matter. You'll achieve and still feel empty. You may go shopping or take a flight to Dubai, a popular destination for those trying to escape, but remember: you have to come down sooner or later. Planes can't fly forever. Life will meet you at baggage claim, holding a sign with your name on it.

Permanent motivation cannot grow in a soul that feels worthless. It doesn't live in hype, hustle, or applause. It lives in dignity. And that means you must be willing to say: *"I matter,"* even when no one else is clapping. That's where the real power is. That's where your future starts.

You were taught that self-worth comes from the car you drive. The world told you that motivation looks like a big house, a six-figure account, designer clothes, and an image polished to perfection. That is the version sold on every screen and echoed in every advertisement.

But that version of motivation is shallow, and that is why it never lasts.

It arrives in quick flashes. It shows up like lightning, exciting for a moment but gone before it can warm anything. It is built on appearance, not depth. That kind of motivation burns fast and burns out even faster. It cannot sustain you because it was never meant to. It was built to impress, not to endure. And what it leaves behind is not satisfaction but emptiness, the kind that asks: *"What now?"* right after the applause fades.

You will never experience permanent motivation if money is what drives you. Wealth, when approached wisely, can be a worthy goal. It can provide freedom, flexibility, and choices. But it should never be the engine that powers your life.

When money becomes the reason you move, instead of the result of meaningful movement, you trade your purpose for a paycheck.

Wealth was meant to serve you, not enslave you. The moment it becomes your master, you begin chasing what should have been moving calmly in your direction.

The things you are meant to achieve in life, peace, impact, and fulfillment, are not fuel; they are fruit. They are the result of discipline, growth, and unwavering focus, not the source of it.

Permanent motivation does not need to shout. It is not loud or flashy. It does not demand recognition or survive on applause. It is steady and rooted in clarity.

When you know who you are and why you are here, the right things are drawn to that certainty. They find you because you are no longer chasing, but becoming.

Meaningful Movement is Permanent Motivation

We chase money, believing it will solve our problems, but money is a tool, not a destination. Like a hammer, it's useful for building something meaningful but useless if you don't know what you're trying to build.

The wealthy often discover this truth too late: financial success without purpose feels hollow.

Consider why lottery winners frequently end up bankrupt and miserable within a few years. They had the money but lacked the internal drive that creates lasting satisfaction. The entrepreneurs who built fortunes, however, often say the money followed naturally once they found work that energized them.

The difference isn't luck or talent alone. It's direction.

Most of us operate like hamsters on a wheel, running faster and faster toward goals others have set for us. We mistake motion for progress. But meaningful work feels different.

When you're solving problems you actually care about, when your skills align with genuine needs, the effort doesn't drain you. It fuels you.

This isn't about abandoning practical concerns or living on dreams alone. Bills need paying. But there's a crucial difference between working for money and letting meaningful work generate money. One leaves you constantly chasing; the other builds something sustainable.

The question isn't whether you deserve success. You do.

The question is whether you're willing to pause long enough to identify what success means to you, separate from what you've been told it should mean.

That clarity becomes your compass.

And everything else is just a path.

Are You Worth It?

"Are you worth it?"

That is the question you must ask yourself. Not casually, not as a throwaway line, but as a serious, soul-searching inquiry. Sit with it. Be still. Listen for the honest answer beneath the voices in your head.

For most people, the answer will come as a quiet, painful *no*. Not because it's true, but because it has been deeply planted. You've been conditioned to believe that your worth is measured by pleasure, not presence. That your value depends on what you produce, how well you perform, or how much approval you can collect.

When Pleasure Replaces Purpose

Over time, pleasure has replaced identity. We've been conditioned to believe that feeling good, even momentarily, validates our worth as human beings.

The culture whispers: *"If something makes you feel desired, wanted, or temporarily significant, then it must be good for you."*

I've watched people remain in toxic, soul-depleting relationships because the fleeting intimacy of physical connection made them feel valued, even if only for moments at a time. Those brief encounters became their evidence of worth.

In the absence of genuine love and respect, they clung to whatever made them feel chosen, even when the person choosing them was ultimately destroying them.

They confused stimulation with significance. They mistook being wanted for being valued. And in doing so, they traded their true worth for temporary affirmation from people who would never see them as more than a momentary pleasure.

This is what happens when we lose touch with our inherent value. We start accepting crumbs of attention as if they were full meals of love. We settle for being someone's escape instead of insisting on being someone's priority. We let fleeting feelings determine our lasting choices, and wonder why we end up empty despite all the temporary highs.

This shows up in the workplace, too. People stay in jobs that slowly drain their spirit, not because they love the work, but because the paycheck keeps the lights on and the air conditioner running.

They confuse survival with stability, and they mistake routine discomfort for responsibility.

But the real question lingers just beneath the surface:

Is comfort worth your life?

Is electricity more valuable than peace of mind?

For those ready to grow, that question hits with clarity. For those still hiding behind fear, it sparks defensiveness.

Many respond with the same reflexive excuse they've used for years: *"What else am I supposed to do?"*

As if the absence of an easy alternative is reason enough to stay trapped.

The truth is, you are not here to survive. You are here to become whole. You are here to stop trading your time, your gifts, and your mental health for a version of safety that slowly kills your purpose.

Staying stuck is not a sign of strength. It is a sign that you've confused sacrifice with surrender.

Your Starting Point

Self-worth is not a luxury reserved for the privileged. It is your starting point. Without it, every decision becomes a negotiation between you and acceptance. Without it, you'll defend dysfunction just because it pays.

And if you don't recognize your value, you'll keep calling bondage a blessing, and wear it like a badge of honor.

The world keeps telling you that fulfillment is somewhere far away. That the Garden of Eden, the fountain of youth, or absolute joy can only be found in some mystical, unreachable place.

But none of that is true.

The truth is much closer than you think. It lives right between your eyes. It always has. You just stopped looking inward.

This inward journey isn't easy. It requires you to examine patterns you've grown comfortable with, relationships you've accepted as normal, and choices you've justified for years.

It means recognizing that some of the pain you carry isn't noble suffering, it's simply familiar. And familiar doesn't mean healthy.

The question isn't whether you're capable of change. You are.

The question is whether you're ready to challenge yourself, to test whether you really believe your life is worth more than the routine that's been draining you.

This isn't theory or motivational slogans. It's an invitation to discover what happens when you stop negotiating with your worth and start building from it instead.

Your value isn't something you need to earn or prove. It's something you need to remember, and act upon.

If you haven't already closed this book, you probably will soon. But if you don't, it means something important has already happened.

It means you've decided what most people never do.

It means you're done pretending you're powerless.

I made this book short and sharp for a reason, so you could read it again and again until something finally breaks through.

Because the truth is, most people will figure out how the pyramids were built before they ever prove that they believe their life is worth changing.

Not because they can't, but because they won't, unless something inside of them finally says: *"Enough."*

Television and other false motivators have trained you to believe that peace, purpose, and power live somewhere far away. In another city. On some distant island. In a future version of yourself that always feels just out of reach.

But that has never been true.

They are right here, right now, already within you.

You've just been distracted long enough to forget.

The world keeps you chasing what you already carry. And most people are too tired or too numb to stop and ask why.

The Familiar Prison

There's a cycle you complain about but never actually leave, a pattern of pain you know so well it feels like home.

Some people aren't addicted to progress, they're addicted to the predictability of their suffering. The known misery feels safer than the unknown possibility of something better.

This isn't weakness. It's human nature. Our minds are wired to choose familiar discomfort over uncertain change, even when that change could lead to genuine fulfillment.

We become archaeologists of our own problems, digging deeper into what's wrong rather than building something new.

When you finally decide to break the pattern, you'll hit resistance. You'll assume it's life pushing back, circumstances conspiring against you, the world telling you no.

But here's what you'll discover: the strongest wall isn't external. It's the part of you that's terrified of becoming someone you don't yet know how to be.

This resistance doesn't mean you're not worth the effort. It means you're human. Your mind is doing exactly what it was designed to do: keep you safe by keeping you the same.

But safe and alive are not the same thing.

And you weren't put here to be safe.

You were put here to grow.

The fact that you're still engaging with these ideas means something important: part of you still believes change is possible. That belief, however small, is where your breakthrough begins, not in the absence of fear, but in your willingness to move forward with it.

The Pain That Opens Doors

Your breakthrough won't come in the absence of fear, but in your willingness to move forward with it.

This resistance you feel isn't your fault. You've been conditioned to interpret any unfamiliar sensation as danger. When you try to change, your nervous system sounds an alarm. The signal is new, so your brain interprets it as a threat. And when something feels threatening, every instinct tells you to retreat.

That's natural. That's human.

But not everything uncomfortable is harmful. Some discomfort is simply the feeling of expansion.

The pain connected to growth fundamentally differs from the pain that warns of damage. Growth pain stretches you toward what you're becoming; pain warns you away from what could destroy you.

Learning to distinguish between them changes everything, because it means you can stop running from the very sensation that signals you're moving in the right direction.

Humanity has always wrestled with why meaningful change must come with discomfort.

Why can't transformation be easy?

Why must we feel the resistance, the fear, the uncertainty?

I believe it's because the process itself makes us stronger. Each time we choose growth over comfort, we reclaim a piece of the power we once possessed naturally.

You were born fearless, curious, and endlessly creative. You believed you could do anything, be anything, become anything.

That wasn't childish naïveté. That was your original nature.

Somewhere along the way, you traded that expansive spirit for the safety of small expectations. You chose survival over possibility.

But those powers aren't lost. They're sleeping.

And every time you move through fear instead of away from it, you wake them up a little more.

What If We Got It Wrong?

Maybe we've misunderstood childhood completely.

What if that fearless creativity we call naïve wasn't childish at all?

What if children who believe they can do anything when they grow up aren't dreaming, they're remembering?

Consider this possibility: the adults who taught us to "be realistic" had their own limitless vision stolen from them, just as they unknowingly stole it from us. Generation after generation, we've been convinced that growing up means growing smaller. That maturity means abandoning the impossible.

But what if the impossible was never impossible?

Think about how children play. They build elaborate forts from pillows and sheets, creating architectural marvels in living rooms. They run through yards with towels tied around their necks, arms outstretched, completely convinced they can fly. Little girls hold full conversations with dolls and stuffed animals, speaking as naturally as if those toys were responding.

We call this imagination.

But what if it's memory?

What if children are accessing something we've forgotten how to see?

What if those pillow fort blueprints are echoes of how the pyramids were really built?

What if that towel-cape flight isn't fantasy but a glimpse of what human potential actually looks like?

What if those conversations with dolls tap into a communication ability we once possessed naturally?

Somewhere in our distant past, something convinced humanity that we were meant to crawl when we were designed to soar. Something made us forget our own capabilities and accept limitation as wisdom.

The question isn't whether this sounds impossible.

The question is: What if we've been living far below what we're actually capable of?

Your childhood dreams weren't too big.

Your adult expectations became too small.

Return to flight, my friends. Return to flight.

The Question behind the Question

Here's a question that cuts to the center of everything: *Are you worth fighting for?*

Not theoretically, not in some inspirational poster way, but practically. When it comes down to the daily choice between comfort and growth, between settling and striving, what do your actions say about how much you value yourself?

Most of us live with a strange contradiction. We know intellectually that we have worth, but we don't act like it. We accept situations that drain us. We tolerate relationships that diminish us. We postpone dreams indefinitely. We say we matter, then treat ourselves as if we don't.

The real question isn't about your inherent worth as a human being. That's not up for debate.

The question is whether you believe your potential is worth the discomfort of pursuing it, whether the person you could become is worth the effort of leaving behind the person you've been.

When you look at your daily choices, your patterns, your compromises, they tell a story about what you truly believe you deserve. Not what you say you deserve, but what you're willing to accept. The gap between those two things reveals everything.

You are worth the fight. Your dreams are worth the risk. Your growth is worth the discomfort.

But knowing that intellectually changes nothing.

Acting like it changes everything.

The question isn't whether you're worth it.

The question is whether you're ready to live like you are.

Reflection Prompt: Are You Really Ready to Change?

Take a quiet moment. No music. No noise. Just honesty.

Answer these questions in a notebook, your phone, or in your heart, but answer them like your life depends on it:

1. Have you ever told yourself, *"This is just the way I am"*?
    What were you avoiding when you said it?
2. What would you lose if you changed?
    Be honest. Sometimes, pain feels safer than growth.
3. If you knew no one would clap for your progress, would you still do it?
    Why or why not?
4. What part of your discomfort are you calling reality?
    Who gave you that version of "real life," and why do

you still follow it?

5. Are you worth it?

   Don't answer quickly. Sit with it. Then write down a new answer you want to believe, even if you don't fully believe it yet.

Chapter One
The Battle For Your Mind

- *"For as he thinketh in his heart, so is he."* (Proverbs 23:7, KJV)
- How negative thought patterns create mental strongholds.
- Neuroscience: the brain's plasticity and ability to change.
- Call to action: recognize the battle and choose your weapons.

The real war isn't out there, it's inside your skull.

Every day, a thousand tiny lies try to take root in your thinking:

- "You're stuck."
- "You're broken."
- "You can't change."

But here's the truth: God wired your mind for renewal, and science backs it up. Your brain can rewire itself through intentional focus and faith.

It's time to stop fighting the wrong battles, and start winning the war that actually matters.

Daily Goal Showers

I've developed a concept called **Daily Goal Showers**.

Just as you shower to cleanse your body, you need to intentionally cleanse your mind, of doubt, stagnation, fear, and the residue of past failures. Mental and spiritual grime

1

builds up from years of negative thought patterns. Without regular cleansing, it clouds your judgment and weighs down your spirit.

Daily Goal Showers aren't abstract ideas. They're tangible, deliberate actions, as essential as brushing your teeth.

Each "shower" might include:

- Writing down three specific goals for the day.
- Spending ten minutes in quiet reflection about your purpose.
- Completing one meaningful task that brings you closer to the person you want to become.

These practices clear away the fog of confusion and rinse off guilt, shame, and self-judgment that you've carried for far too long.

Here's a crucial mindset shift: **goals are not points scored against others.**

If you see personal transformation as a competition with someone else, you've missed the point. Whether you're pursuing spiritual growth, financial stability, physical wellness, or stronger relationships, the only competitor is the person you were yesterday.

That's the only benchmark that matters.

Daily Goal Showers are **spiritual hygiene**.

Every time you act intentionally, every time you check in with your purpose instead of drifting through your day, you declare:

"I matter. I'm worth the discipline."

These are not just routines. They are acts of **self-respect** in a world that profits from your chaos and confusion.

But this practice also confronts a question most people avoid: *Do I believe I'm worth the effort?*

It's easier to stay distracted than to sit in the discomfort of possibly deserving peace, growth, and fulfillment. The mirror of daily intention doesn't just reflect what you want to do, it reflects whether you truly believe you deserve to do it.

Some people won't even call peace "desirable." They'll label it boring, unproductive, unnatural.

They've been conditioned to crave drama and dysfunction, to find identity in the adrenaline of pain.

"Pleasurable pain" begins to sound more appealing than "graceful peace."

And that's not poetic metaphor; it's a psychological trap.

Chaos has become familiar. Peace feels foreign.

But peace isn't passive. Peace is **power**. It's not the absence of motion, it's the **presence of clarity**.

When you commit to Daily Goal Showers, you're not just washing away doubt, fear, and pain.

You're reminding your soul what it's worth.

And if that feels uncomfortable, **good**. That means you're waking up. That means you're getting clean.

Why Change Feels Impossible

This book is fundamentally about **change**. But let's be honest, change might be the single hardest thing a human being ever attempts.

Even when we know we desperately need it. Even when staying the same is slowly destroying us.

So, why is something so essential **so difficult**?

I believe it comes down to three barriers most people never confront:

1. *We don't believe we're worth the effort change requires.*
2. *We've become disconnected from others and lost the motivation that comes from being needed.*
3. *Change demands energy and hope, resources many feel they no longer possess.*

These barriers reinforce one another.

When you don't believe you're worth saving, you stop building the relationships that could support your growth.

When you're isolated, change feels pointless, there's no one to change for.

When you're exhausted from years of mere survival, transformation sounds overwhelming instead of exciting.

But here's the truth that shatters all three barriers:

The question isn't whether you're **capable** of change. *You are.* The question isn't whether others would benefit from your growth. *They would.*

The real question is: *Are you ready to believe that a better version of yourself is not only possible, but inevitable, once you stop fighting your own potential?*

Change is hard because it asks you to act like you matter **before** you feel like you matter.

It requires you to invest in someone you haven't met yet, the future version of you.

Value this moment. It's the most courageous act a human can perform.

***

I've seen people make companions of their pain, nursing old wounds with a tenderness they deny themselves in every other area of life.

They build fortresses of suffering, believing that their scars somehow make them safe.

But what they don't realize is this: *Pain, when held too long and too closely, becomes a prison.*

It masquerades as wisdom when it's actually just fear, dressed in familiar clothes.

There is a difference between the peace that comes from **healing**, and the silence that comes from **giving up**.

One is a **doorway**.

The other is a **wall**.

Yet we convince ourselves that the wall protects us. That our isolation is noble. That refusing to hope is realism, not tragedy.

But to ask yourself *honestly* if you are worth the fight, and then to wait for an honest answer, **that** requires a courage most people spend a lifetime avoiding.

Because if the answer is yes, and it always is, then you have to live like it.

Living accordingly means leaving the fortress built from your wounds and walking into the light you've been avoiding.

Living without purpose is a quiet form of exile.

You blend into the noise of the world, pretending that comfort can be found inside your distractions.

But that isn't life. That's slow survival.

You stop showing up.

You stop dreaming.

You build walls and call it healing.

But deep down, you know you've disappeared.

So don't ask God if you're worth saving.

Ask yourself.

That's the question that matters most.

Do you believe your story is still worth telling?

Because if you don't, no amount of motivation will stick.

Your answer becomes your **ceiling**, or your **starting line**.

Here's the truth: *You were never disqualified.*

You just stopped believing you were still in the fight.

But the fact that you're reading this means, you haven't quit.

The fact that it still hurts means, you're still alive.

***

◀ Reflection Exercise: Are You Worth It?

Don't answer quickly. Sit with it. This isn't about pretending, it's about deciding.

1. Write down your honest answer to this question:

Do I believe I'm worth saving, healing, rebuilding, and rising?

Write your answer in a complete sentence, even if it feels painful, angry, or uncertain.

2. Who told you that you weren't worth it?

Make a list, not to blame, but to name.

These could be people, systems, moments, or internal voices that fed the lie.

3. What evidence have you lived by that proves you believed the lie?

Think about the risks you didn't take, the dreams you shelved, the comfort you chose instead of growth.

4. Now flip the script:

Write a statement of truth, not fake hype, but faith-based fact.

"I am still here. I am still breathing. That means I am

still called."

"I've been down, but I'm not out. My story isn't finished."

5. Final declaration:

Copy this or rewrite your own version:

"I am worth the fight. I will not disappear into the comfort of pain. I choose life. I choose growth. I choose to believe what God has already said about me."

The First Sin

We sin against ourselves first, long before we rebel against God.

We betray our worth.

We silence our voice.

We lower our standards and call it humility.

But it's not humility, it's spiritual neglect.

That's where the fall begins: not with disobedience, but with disbelief.

And disbelief whispers,

"I'm not worth the life God gave me."

This question of worth isn't just difficult, it's embarrassing.

Because if you're honest, you've probably been living below your calling for a while.

Not because you weren't capable.

Not because God said no.

But because you stopped believing in what was possible.

And nothing paralyzes a dream faster than self-betrayal.

Here's the truth that cuts through every excuse: If you're not living your most healed, useful, impactful life, it's not because it's impossible. It's because you haven't chosen it yet.

That may sound harsh, but it's the only way forward. Truth is the doorway to transformation.

If you haven't chosen your highest self, there are only two reasons: Either you don't believe that life belongs to you, Or you've decided you're not worth the effort it requires.

Both are forms of the same spiritual rebellion, the refusal to honor what God created you to become.

But if that's where you find yourself, stuck between disbelief and avoidance, then this is your invitation to remember:

Your life is your vote of confidence in divine possibility. Your actions are your answer to the question of your own worth.

And as long as you have breath in your lungs, you still get to choose.

Choose differently.

Choose boldly.

Choose like someone who knows they were created for more than survival.

The Question We Avoid

The fact that "Can I change?" is even a question that needs to be asked is a tragedy in itself. Most people would rather distract themselves than sit still long enough to answer it.

But it's one of the most important confrontations you'll ever have, and the answers aren't always comfortable.

Here's what makes this question so difficult: We live in a world that has normalized exhaustion and neglect.

Walk through any workplace, any neighborhood, any family gathering, and you'll see people who look depleted. Not because they don't care about themselves, but because they're overwhelmed just trying to survive.

People are working longer hours, carrying more stress, and shouldering heavier burdens than their bodies and minds were designed to handle.

They're not lazy, they're overloaded and under-supported.

While some enjoy the luxury of home gyms, meditation retreats, and restorative vacations, millions of others skip meals, sacrifice sleep, and push through pain because the system demands it.

When that kind of pressure becomes normal, **self-care becomes the first casualty**. And when self-care disappears, self-worth isn't far behind.

You start to believe that your value exists only in your productivity, your worth only in your output.

This is why asking, *"Are you worth it?"* feels so

uncomfortable. Because somewhere along the way, many of us stopped believing the answer was *yes*. We accepted that our health was optional, our peace was a luxury we couldn't afford, and our well-being was less important than everyone else's demands.

But here's what the world won't tell you:

You are not your labor.

You are not your schedule.

You are not your bank account or your productivity metrics.

You are worth the care you keep giving to everything and everyone else.

The question isn't whether you can afford to prioritize your worth.

The question is whether you can afford **not to**.

The Battle You Don't Know You're Fighting

The mental stress the world inflicts on the average person isn't the kind that gets diagnosed. It's the kind that gets ignored, dismissed as normal. accepted as the price of modern living.

Because most people don't realize their minds are being systematically hijacked. They're taught to distract, avoid, scroll, overwork, and overeat just to stay out of their own heads.

This isn't accidental. There's an unspoken alliance between the forces that profit from your attention and those that profit from your labor.

Social media companies need you scrolling. Employers need you exhausted. Entertainment industries need you escaping. Consumer culture needs you spending.

They all benefit when you're too distracted, too tired, or too numb to question the life you're actually living.

The result? Most people become strangers to themselves. They don't trust their own thoughts, their memories, or even their silence.

When faced with the prospect of being alone with themselves, they panic and reach for another distraction.

This fear of self-encounter runs so deep that the mind creates defense mechanisms to avoid it entirely.

Your subconscious, trying to protect you from what it perceives as the threat of authentic self-reflection, builds a counterfeit identity.

It tells you to chase status, stay busy, and focus on everyone else's problems.

This false self feels safer because it's constructed from external validation rather than internal truth.

But this isn't protection, it's disconnection. And disconnection doesn't preserve; it slowly poisons.

When you finally sit still long enough to listen, you start to notice how many fears and limiting beliefs you've accepted as permanent parts of your identity:

"I'm just anxious."

"I'M not creative."

"I'm bad with money."

These aren't facts about who you are, they're survival strategies you adopted to navigate a world that never taught you how to come home to yourself.

Permanent motivation doesn't come from external change or endless self-improvement techniques.

It emerges when you learn to return to your authentic self, without fear of what you'll discover there.

The real work isn't fixing what's wrong with you. It's recognizing what was never actually you to begin with.

Throwing Out What Isn't You

You won't see your real reflection until you hold yourself to the light. When you do, the false identities start to fade, and your authentic self begins to emerge.

This process isn't about fixing what's wrong with you, it's about discarding what was never truly you to begin with.

You can't repair what doesn't belong, because the mind doesn't work that way. Your psyche naturally rejects foreign elements that don't align with your true nature. It's designed to handle genuine challenges like illness, loss, or natural hardship. But it struggles under the weight of artificial pressures because those forces are fundamentally unnatural.

Consider what your mind was never meant to process:

- constant comparison through social media,
- perpetual availability through technology,
- artificial scarcity created by consumer culture,
- and the relentless pressure to optimize every aspect of your existence.

These aren't natural human challenges, they're manufactured stressors that exploit vulnerabilities in our psychology.

Your mind functions best when you maintain control over your own thoughts, decisions, and direction. But when you surrender that control to external forces, when you let algorithms dictate what you see, employers define your worth, or social expectations shape your goals, your mental clarity becomes compromised.

The solution isn't to fight harder against these unnatural pressures. It's to recognize them as foreign invaders, and systematically remove them from your life.

Stop trying to adapt to systems that were never designed for your wellbeing. Start building a life that aligns with how your mind actually works: with purpose, autonomy, and authentic connection.

When you reclaim control of your mental environment, you don't have to fix yourself. You simply need to clear away everything that isn't truly you, and let your real self rise to the surface.

Breaking the Pain Response

A mind used by others is a mind used against its owner. When external forces control your thoughts, change becomes the enemy. You hear yourself saying:

"I have no time to change."

"It's pointless."

"I've tried this before."

What you're actually doing is reinforcing the lie that keeps you trapped.

That hesitation you feel when you try to act on something good? That instant resistance that makes you recoil from positive action? That's your pain response, a trained reflex designed to keep you exactly where you are.

It's not logic. It's not wisdom. It's conditioning that mistakes growth for danger.

But here's what the pain response doesn't want you to know: **It can be broken.** Like any reflex, it loses power when you understand how it works and refuse to obey it automatically.

The discomfort you feel when taking positive action is temporary. It's your nervous system sounding a false alarm, treating the unfamiliar as threatening. But on the other side of that discomfort lies something lasting: clarity, confidence, and the deep satisfaction that comes from choosing growth over safety.

Every time you act despite the resistance, you're training a new response.

Every small step toward change weakens the old programming.

Every moment you choose progress over comfort, you're rewiring your mind to recognize growth as natural, not dangerous.

Don't overthink it.

Don't wait to feel ready.

The pain response feeds on hesitation and grows

stronger with delay.

Act now. Move now. Do something, anything, that signals to your nervous system that you're still committed to becoming who you're meant to be.

Your breakthrough isn't waiting for perfect conditions. It's waiting for you to stop letting a false alarm system run your life.

"Call to Action"

Daily Goal Showers: Your Mental Cleansing Routine

Before you chase new goals, cleanse your mental atmosphere. Your external world mirrors your internal world. If your environment is filled with chaos and negativity, your mind will reflect that instability.

Here's how to implement your daily cleansing practice:

Step 1: Clear Your Environment

Remove every consistently negative voice from your life. This includes:

- friends who drain your energy,
- critics who mock your vision,
- and people who celebrate your failures more than your progress.

You don't need their permission to grow, their approval to change, or their presence to succeed.

Start small if necessary. Limit your exposure gradually, but be intentional about protecting your mental space from people who profit from your doubt

Step 2: Reprogram Your Internal Voice

Your inner dialogue isn't fixed. It's programmable, and **you** are the programmer.

Begin each day by consciously choosing what your internal voice will focus on. Replace shame-based thoughts with truth-based ones. Counter doubt with reminders of your past successes, however small.

Make your inner voice your strongest advocate, not your harshest critic. This takes practice, but it's the most important conversation you'll ever change.

Step 3: Acknowledge Your Progress

Celebrate that you're taking action, even if progress feels slow. Recognize how far you've come, even if it's just inches rather than miles. Don't wait for external applause to validate your growth.

Write down three things you've accomplished today, no matter how minor they seem. Progress compounds when you start to notice it.

Step 4: Establish Your Foundation

Build your days on three principles that can't be shaken by circumstances:

- **Grace** – You are enough, even when you fall short. Mistakes don't define your worth.
- **Peace** – You don't need to prove your value through constant striving. Your worth isn't performance-based.

- **Abundance** – True prosperity starts in your mindset before it shows up in your bank account.

The Key Truth

Changing your environment is often easier than changing your internal patterns, which is why we start there. But once you clean both your external and internal space, you create the conditions where genuine transformation becomes possible.

Your daily goal shower isn't just about setting intentions. It's about systematically removing everything that keeps you from seeing clearly and acting boldly on what truly matters.

The War Within

The self is the only enemy that matters in this war.

It knows every weakness, every scar, every escape route you've ever used. It whispers doubt at the exact moment you try to rise. It doesn't need to sabotage you loudly, just consistently.

This enemy won't come from the outside. It lives in your thoughts. And unless you face it, you'll keep losing battles no one else can see.

This version of the self isn't your soul or your true nature. It's the untrained self, the part of you shaped by fear, disappointment, and the lies you've absorbed from a broken world.

It's the voice that says "not today" every time you try to grow. It's the internal drag that calls consistency a waste of time and dreams unrealistic.

This enemy isn't unbeatable, it's just familiar. And familiarity has fooled you into accepting its voice as truth.

You don't defeat this enemy through brute force or willpower alone. You defeat it through exposure.

You shine light on the lies it tells.

You challenge the patterns it repeats.

You set goals and show up for them, even when your hands shake with resistance.

Every act of discipline becomes an act of defiance against the false self. Every time you finish what you start, your true self grows stronger, and its voice becomes clearer.

This isn't self-help. It's **spiritual warfare**.

The battlefield is your mind, and the victory determines who you become.

So if you're looking for someone to fight, don't look out the window. Look in the mirror.

Then do something revolutionary: **forgive that version of yourself.**

Train it.

Challenge it.

Love it enough to stop obeying it.

Your dreams don't need permission from your past. They need leadership from your present.

And that leadership begins the moment you stop surrendering to the self that fears your future, and start building the self that believes in it.

Weekly Goal Shower: A Spiritual Reset

The weekly goal shower is more than a routine, it's renewal. It's the conscious decision to wash off what's not yours: shame, fear, false identities, and inherited limitations. It's your return to the truth of who you are beneath all the noise.

Set aside one intentional time each week, even just 15 to 20 minutes, to sit, reflect, and realign with your authentic self.

Step 1: Spiritual Cleanse: What am I carrying that isn't mine?

Write down the thoughts, labels, comparisons, fears, or obligations that didn't originate from your true nature. These are the mental burdens you've picked up from external pressure, past experiences, or other people's expectations.

Cross them out one by one. As you do, say aloud or silently: **"This is not my burden. I release it."**

This isn't your shame to carry. It isn't your responsibility to manage other people's emotions. It isn't your job to live up to someone else's definition of success.

Step 2: Renewal Reading: One truth to absorb

Choose a piece of wisdom that speaks to transformation and renewal. This might be:

- A meaningful quote from a book that's impacted you
- A line of poetry that captures your aspirations
- A personal affirmation you've written
- A spiritual text that resonates with your beliefs

Sit with these words. Read them slowly. Let them penetrate beyond surface understanding. This isn't casual reading; it's the intentional absorption of truth that can reshape your thinking.

Step 3: Mental Mirror: Who was I this week? Who am I becoming?

Identify one thought pattern or reaction that pulled you back into fear, doubt, or old limitations this week. Don't judge it. Observe it with curiosity.

Then write down one specific way you will respond differently next time, even if it's just a small adjustment. This isn't self-criticism; it's alignment practice. You're training yourself to recognize when you're operating from your authentic self versus your conditioned responses.

Step 4: Your Worth Statement

Complete this sentence in writing: **"This week reminded me that I am worth _____, and I will not forget it."**

Examples:

- "...peace, even when everything around me is chaotic."
- "...saying no to what drains my energy."
- "...following through on commitments I make to myself."
- "...pursuing dreams that others don't understand."

Write it down. Your worth needs to be declared, not just felt. And you need to hear yourself say it, especially when the world tries to convince you otherwise.

***

● *Renewal Reading One scripture to soak in*

Pick one of the following, or use your own:

- **Romans 12:2**: *"Be transformed by the renewing of your mind..."*
- **Isaiah 43:19**: *"Behold, I will do a new thing..."*
- **John 15:3**: *"Now ye are clean through the word..."*

Sit with the verse. Say it slowly. Let it reach your spirit. This is not just reading, it's rinsing.

***

🙏 Optional Ending Prayer:

"God, cleanse my thoughts. Clear my vision. Strengthen my heart. Let me walk into this next week with clean hands, a sound mind, and a permanent fire in my spirit. I am not my failures. I am not my fear. I am Yours, and that's more than enough."

The Beast Within

The untrained self is the giant you face every day. It towers over your aspirations with the weight of past failures, inherited shame, and every voice that ever told you what you couldn't become. This isn't the enemy outside your door; it's the one that lives in your thoughts, knows your every weakness, and strikes at the exact moment you try to rise.

You've been fighting this giant with the wrong

equipment. We all have. We've armed ourselves with other people's strategies and wrapped ourselves in emotional armor that was never designed for our specific battle.

This armor looks impressive from the outside, made of external validation, defensive mechanisms, and coping strategies that numb pain instead of healing it. But it's heavy, unfamiliar, and ultimately useless against an enemy that attacks from within.

The problem isn't that you're not strong enough. The problem is that you're fighting an internal battle with external tools.

Self-help books, motivational videos, quick fixes, and surface-level solutions can't reach the depths where this giant lives. They're like bringing a sword to fight something that exists in your soul.

You need a different approach entirely, not more weapons, but a fundamental shift in how you understand the battle itself.

The giant isn't conquered through force; it is transformed through truth. Every lie it tells about your worth must be countered with evidence of who you really are. Every limiting belief it whispers needs to be replaced with possibility you're willing to act on

This isn't about destroying parts of yourself. It's about training the untrained, healing the wounded, and teaching the fearful aspects of your mind to serve your highest good instead of sabotaging it.

The victory doesn't come from becoming someone else. It comes from becoming fully, authentically yourself, the person who was always there beneath the giant's shadow, waiting for you to remember your true strength.

Remember, David rejected Saul's armor because he didn't trust it. He had never tested it. And that's the key to fighting self.

As stated before, you don't need new weapons, you need divine intervention. You've already tried everything else, and none of it worked. In fact, most of it made the pain worse.

The Power of Surrender

To truly defeat the untrained self, you must drop the weapons that haven't been working. Reject the war mentality and surrender to a different approach entirely.

This isn't giving up, it's giving in to what actually works: alignment over achievement, purpose over productivity, and presence over performance.

Daily goal showers become your soul-scrubbing rituals, committed to each day not to impress others or compete in some imaginary race, but to stay connected to what actually matters to you.

A meaningful goal doesn't have to be monumental. It can be as practical as learning a new skill, mastering a recipe that brings you joy, or taking ten minutes of complete stillness to reconnect with your deeper self.

But here's the key: when you choose a goal, sit with it. Let it breathe. Practice it consistently for at least three days before moving on. Let it take root in your life rather than treating it like another item to check off and forget.

Too many of us are drowning in productivity while starving for purpose. We jump from app to app, strategy to strategy, hoping something will finally make us feel complete. But if you constantly feel like you're not doing enough, you're probably doing too much of the wrong things.

The antidote isn't more activity, it's more intentionality.

Slow down. Breathe. Remember that you are not late to your own life. You didn't miss your window of opportunity. There is no cosmic leaderboard where your worth gets calculated against someone else's progress.

The only moment you fall behind is the moment you look sideways and start measuring your path against someone else's journey. That's when discouragement takes root. That's when anxiety grows legs and starts running your decisions.

But what's meant for you cannot be stolen, delayed, or derailed by another person's timeline.

Your arrival is always right on time. Stay in your lane, move at your pace, and trust that surrendering to your authentic path is the most powerful victory you can achieve.

What Really Matters

Let go of what people think about your image, the shallow judgments, the surface-level assumptions, the commentary on your appearance or possessions. Those things have nothing to do with your worth. But never stop caring about what people think of your character, your integrity, and the imprint your spirit leaves on the world. Because that's the part of you that speaks when you're not in the room. That's the true fruit of who you are.

It is a sad life to obsess over how others perceive your image. It is a liberated life to walk in the quiet strength of integrity. The world may see your car, job title, and social media presence. But the people who truly matter, and your own conscience, know how you show up. They observe how you treat those who can't do anything for you. They feel the energy you bring into every room.

A marathon runner is called a runner not because he owns the right gear or looks the part, but because he runs. His movement defines him. It is consistent action, not commentary from the sidelines, that gives him his identity. Whether people admire his form or question his pace is irrelevant. He runs, and that commitment to discipline shapes who he is.

Your character works the same way. It is built through your daily choices, your responses to challenges, and your treatment of others when no one is watching. Opinions about your image will shift with every trend and season, but your integrity creates a foundation that can't be shaken by external judgment.

Focus on becoming someone you respect, regardless of who's paying attention. Real confidence comes not from managing perceptions but from knowing you are living in alignment with your deepest values.

Purpose over Pressure

Your concern shouldn't be the commentary from the sidelines. Focus on how you're living in the arena. It's not about what people think of your performance, it's about what they witness through your character. Your conduct, your persistence, your integrity under pressure, that's what tells the real story.

Here's the problem most of us face: we're gorging ourselves on activity while starving for actual purpose. We've become addicted to doing but allergic to simply being. We chase goals without clear direction, confuse frantic motion for genuine momentum, and exhaust ourselves running toward destinations that were never ours to begin with.

This is why so many people feel lost despite being constantly busy. They pursue outcomes they think they want instead of engaging in work that truly fulfills them. Money becomes the destination instead of what it really is, a tool that flows naturally when you're aligned with your true purpose.

You can't reach a place that doesn't exist. If you make external validation or financial accumulation your primary destination, you'll spend your entire life in motion but never experience arrival. It's like trying to hold your breath permanently, what's meant to flow naturally becomes deadly when you try to trap and control it.

The deeper issue is fear masquerading as practicality. People aren't afraid of trying something meaningful, they're afraid that even after genuine effort, they might fail and confirm their worst suspicions about themselves. So they avoid the risk entirely, choosing familiar dissatisfaction over uncertain possibility.

But here's what that fear-based thinking misses: the effort itself transforms you, regardless of the outcome. Hard work aligned with purpose shapes character, builds confidence, and teaches you to be fully present in your own life. You don't need to conquer the entire mountain today. You just need to show up consistently on the path.

When you're truly engaged in meaningful work, work that serves something larger than immediate comfort, you become present. And presence is where your real power lives, not in the approval of spectators or the accumulation of external rewards.

What You Really Want

Look deeper than your stated goals. Beneath the drive for success is a cry for relief. Relief from the pressure of unpaid bills. Relief from constantly having to prove your worth. Relief from pretending to be someone you're not just to survive in a world that feels increasingly hostile to authentic living.

Most people aren't actually seeking riches, they're seeking rest. But we've been conditioned to believe that rest must be earned through exhaustion, that we can only sleep peacefully after we've hustled ourselves into the ground, that peace is a luxury available only to those who've paid the right price in suffering.

This is the trap that keeps so many people running on empty. They chase external wealth, hoping it will buy them internal peace, not realizing that the peace they're seeking was never for sale in the first place.

Real abundance begins when you stop chasing what you think you should want and start aligning with what you actually need. It starts when you recognize that the relief you're seeking doesn't come from accumulating more, it comes from releasing what's not essential. It emerges when you stop trading your authentic self for someone else's definition of success.

Here's what happens when you make this shift: you discover the real high everyone is unconsciously chasing. It's not the car, the money, or the social media followers. It's that inner explosion of possibility that occurs when you're truly aligned with your purpose. No external achievement, no temporary pleasure, no shallow validation can match the energy that flows through you when you're living authentically.

When genuine motivation hits, the kind that comes from internal alignment rather than external pressure, you feel more alive, more capable, more like the person you were always meant to be. This isn't just a temporary feeling. It's the beginning of becoming who you actually are beneath all the roles and expectations you've been carrying.

The secret is staying connected to that authentic energy rather than letting it get buried under new pressures and old patterns. When you do, you don't just feel different, you become different. And that transformation is the real wealth you were seeking all along.

When Everything Aligns

The confidence is real. The vision becomes clearer. Your body responds with more energy, better posture, deeper breathing. This isn't motivational hype or temporary excitement. This is what alignment feels like when it moves from concept to lived experience.

Your cells begin to act like they believe you. Your nervous system stops fighting against your goals and starts supporting them. Your mind stops generating excuses and starts generating solutions. This is the permanent state where you want to live, not as a peak experience you visit occasionally, but as your natural way of being.

This is what you've been seeking underneath all the external goals: the feeling of being fully alive in your own life, completely aligned with who you're meant to become. This is permanent motivation.

The Divine Spark Within

The rush of sudden motivation is not random. It is not meaningless. It echoes the first act of creation itself. When you feel that surge, that explosion of possibility inside your spirit, you're experiencing a reflection of the moment life itself burst into existence. Creativity is proof that you carry something divine within you, an invisible connection to the source of all creation: God.

Many people shy away from acknowledging this profound experience. We've been conditioned to dismiss such moments as mere chemical reactions or wishful thinking. But every time someone creates, loves deeply, protects what matters, or builds something beautiful from nothing, they participate in an act of divine birthing. Every person, whether they understand it or not, has given birth countless times through their mind, their work, and their dreams.

The soul resides near the core of your being. That's why you feel gut instincts and why your stomach drops in moments of danger or awe. True motivation rises from this same sacred center. It bubbles up from the depths, not from the surface chatter of your thoughts. but from the wellspring of your deepest self.

When you are genuinely motivated, not by external pressure but by internal calling, there is an explosion of life force inside you. This is not random energy or foolish enthusiasm. This is divine power choosing to move through you, the creative force of existence expressing itself in your unique gifts and vision.

Most people chase this transcendent feeling without realizing what they're actually seeking. They pursue money, approval, status, and achievement, but what they truly crave is that primal sensation of life bursting open inside them. They are desperate for the reminder that they are alive for a sacred purpose: they were created to create. And this is how you become permanently motivated.

This is your invitation to recognize these moments of divine inspiration not as fleeting highs to chase but as calls to participate consciously in the ongoing act of creation that flows through all existence.

Living in Your Power

This feeling of divine creativity isn't weakness or wishful thinking. It's pure power. It's your spirit waging war against death, against apathy, against the slow suffocation of settling for less than you're capable of. To be permanently motivated is to be fully alive. To create consistently is to conquer the forces that would keep you small.

If you have ever felt that surge, that electric moment where possibilities opened wide before you and the future felt limitless, you have touched something transcendent.

You've tasted what it means to operate from your true power rather than your conditioned limitations.

But here's what most people miss: you're not supposed to live for occasional flashes of that feeling. You're meant to make it your natural state.

Sustained motivation isn't about maintaining artificial excitement or forcing enthusiasm you don't feel. It's the disciplined practice of staying connected to what gives your life meaning. It's choosing to engage with work that matters to you, relationships that energize rather than drain you, and goals that spring from your authentic desires rather than external expectations.

This connection becomes your anchor through inevitable storms, periods of loneliness, moments of fear, and temporary setbacks. Not because you become invulnerable to life's challenges, but because you remain plugged into something larger than your immediate circumstances. You remember that your creative capacity connects you to the same force that brings everything meaningful into existence.

When you live from this place of sustained connection to your creative power, you stop experiencing motivation as something that comes and goes randomly. Instead, it becomes the steady current that powers your daily choices, your long-term vision, and your ability to contribute something meaningful to the world.

This is permanent motivation. So stop chasing peak moments and start building a life that naturally generates the energy, purpose, and creative satisfaction you've been seeking.

From Red Bull to Clear River

We have become a Red Bull society instead of a clear-river society. We rely on artificial stimulants, external motivation, and temporary energy boosts to keep us moving. But rivers run without stopping toward their destinations, and no outside motivation is needed. Rivers are permanently motivated because they remain connected to their source.

This is the secret of sustainable motivation: connection to something larger than temporary circumstances. When you're plugged into your authentic purpose, your original source, you don't need constant external fuel to keep moving. The energy flows naturally from within.

Here's the question that reveals everything: What kind of river are you?

Some rivers flow directly to the ocean, maintaining their individual path with singular focus until they reach their ultimate destination. These are the people who identify their life's work early and pursue it with unwavering dedication, never allowing distractions to pull them off course.

Other rivers flow into larger rivers, joining their waters with a greater current that eventually reaches the ocean. These are the people who find their purpose by supporting someone else's vision, contributing their unique gifts to a larger mission, and reaching their destination through collaboration rather than individual achievement.

Both paths lead to the same place, the vast ocean of fulfilled potential. Both are necessary. Both have power. The key is knowing which type of river you are and flowing accordingly, rather than fighting against your natural current.

If you're a direct-to-ocean river, protect your singular focus. Don't let others convince you to merge prematurely or abandon your unique path for someone else's journey.

If you're a tributary river, find the right current to join. Surround yourself with people whose vision aligns with your values and whose direction matches your destination. Your contribution to their flow doesn't diminish you; it amplifies your impact.

The mistake is trying to be the wrong type of river or flowing with currents that move in the opposite direction from your true destination. Know your nature. Trust your flow. Stay connected to your source. And let that connection carry you naturally toward where you're meant to be.

Daily Reminders: Living in Permanent Motivation

The River Within

Permanent motivation is not a one-time event, it's a river flowing beneath the surface of your life. Most people never dig deep enough to find it, so they live dehydrated and desperate. But once you find it, truly find it, you can tap into it again and again. The river never runs dry. Only your courage to dig does.

Action before Feeling

The biggest lie you've been told is that you need to feel motivated in order to act. No. You act because you are connected to something deeper than temporary emotions. You move because you know the river is there, even when you can't feel it today. Faith moves first; feelings follow later.

Clarity over Hustle

Your spirit doesn't need more hustle, it needs clarity. Motivation rises from clarity the way the sun rises from the horizon. No sun, no life. No clarity, no sustainable action. Stop grinding without purpose and start living with intention.

Creation as Rebellion

Every act of creation you perform is a rebellion against despair. When you write, build, love, plan, or take meaningful risks, you shout into the darkness: *"I will not quit."* You refuse to die unrealized. Permanent motivation is prayer with your feet moving.

Expansion over Survival

You were never created to grind for mere survival. You were created to live for expansion, to move, breathe, and create freely without apology. When you're truly connected to your purpose, your work flows and feeds you rather than draining you.

Honor the Whisper

When motivation surges, it demands a response. Ignore it too many times, and it fades. Honor it, and it grows stronger. Learn to move when inspiration whispers. Don't wait until life has to shout. Permanent motivation is the skill of hearing the quiet call and acting immediately.

Discipline over Feeling

Motivation is not a feeling, it's a discipline. Feelings

come and go. Emotions rise and fall. But motivation, as a spiritual practice, produces a harvest that cannot be stolen by fear or fatigue.

Purpose over Adrenaline

Connection to your purpose is stronger than any adrenaline rush. Adrenaline fades quickly, but purpose builds lasting stamina. True motivation isn't frantic energy, it's focused fire. The steady flame burns for a lifetime, while the quick flare dies out by Monday.

Reflection Exercise: Tapping into Permanent Motivation

Before moving forward, stop and reflect on these five truths:

1. **Where does your deepest motivation come from?**
   (Is it fear? Approval? Or is it connection to something bigger than you?)
2. **When have you felt the surge of true life energy in your soul?**
   (Write down a moment you felt truly alive, creative, or fearless.)

3. **What daily habits are helping you stay connected to your Source?**
   (Identify and protect these habits like a sacred garden.)

4. **Who or what has been throwing buckets of water on your fire?**
   (Name the distractions. Remove them ruthlessly.)

5. **What one small creation will you birth today?**
   (A conversation, a plan, an idea, an act of service, small seeds lead to massive trees.)

The Power of Sacred Speech

Prayer is the return of divine breath. It is not an act of begging or pleading; it is the natural response of a soul still connected to its Source. If you were breathed into existence by the creative force of the universe, then every time you speak with intention, every time you pray, affirm, or declare, you are releasing that same creative power. Your words hold the ability to reshape not just your circumstances but your very understanding of who you are.

You do not speak things into existence because you learned a technique. You speak things into existence because you carry divine creative capacity within you. You were formed by the same intelligence that shapes galaxies and seasons, and you were infused with the spark of that creative force. Every word that falls from your lips is either building your life or diminishing it. Choose to build. Choose to breathe life into your dreams, your relationships, and your vision of who you're becoming.

The question is whether you believe you're worth fighting for. If you recognize your inherent value, these insights become tools of transformation in your hands. If you believe you're not worth the effort, you'll set aside this wisdom and return to the familiar patterns that keep you small. But here's the truth: you are absolutely worth fighting for. You are both the battleground where this transformation happens and the victory that emerges from it.

Release yourself from any system or voice that made you feel perpetually inadequate. Say goodbye to ideologies that lied to you about your value. Disconnect from the opinions of people who barely understand their own worth, let alone yours. Your value was established by the creative force that brought you into being. No human institution, no cultural message, no personal history has ever had the authority to redefine what you're truly worth.

You carry within you the same creative power that speaks worlds into existence. Use it wisely. Use it boldly. Use it to declare the truth of who you're becoming rather than the lies about who you've been told you are.

The Creative Power of Thought

"As a man thinketh in his heart, so is he." This ancient wisdom points to an incredible truth we've largely forgotten: our thoughts have creative power.

Yet if this is true, why aren't we seeing more miraculous transformations? The answer is both simple and profound: we are constantly creating, but most of our mental energy goes toward negative creation. We think ourselves into anxiety, limitation, and doubt with the same power we could use to think ourselves into possibility, abundance, and growth. Our creative capacity is being used against us rather than for us.

Every persistent worry is an act of creation, you imagine

and rehearse unwanted outcomes until they feel real. Every limiting belief you repeat creates mental barriers to your own potential. Every time you say, *"I can't," "It's impossible,"* or *"I'm not good enough,"* you're using your creative power to reinforce limitations.

This is why positive thinking alone isn't enough. You can't simply add positive thoughts to a foundation of negative mental patterns and expect transformation. You must first recognize and interrupt the negative creation process already running in your mind's background.

Here's the practical path forward: instead of trying to believe something will happen, practice the feeling of already having it. When you set a goal, don't spend your mental energy hoping and wishing. Instead, spend it experiencing, in your imagination, what it feels like to have already achieved what you want.

This isn't wishful thinking; it's mental rehearsal. Athletes visualize successful performance before competition. Successful people mentally rehearse achievement before it happens physically. You're training your mind to recognize and move toward what you want rather than what you fear.

The creative power of your thoughts is real, but it requires intentional direction. Stop using it accidentally to create what you don't want, and start using it deliberately to create what you do want. Your mind is already creating your reality. The question is whether you're going to direct that process consciously or let it run on autopilot.

The Mental Aspect of Self-Respect

Forgive yourself for your past. Forgive yourself not because you were right, but because you deserve freedom. Every day, look your mistakes in the eye and then choose to turn your back on them. True forgiveness isn't pretending you did nothing wrong; it's burying what's dead with dignity and choosing to live among the living.

You are not erasing responsibility when you forgive yourself. You are fulfilling it. You are not becoming selfish. You are becoming wise. Wisdom says, *"This happened. I learned. I buried it. It will not rise again."* And when those old voices of shame try to resurrect the past, wisdom answers, *"That chapter is closed."*

This act of self-forgiveness becomes the foundation for something even more essential: unshakable dignity. When you stop punishing yourself for past mistakes, you create space for self-respect to take root. Self-respect isn't a luxury reserved for people with perfect lives; it is the inner light that keeps you standing when everything else falls apart.

Dignity remains when the bills are unpaid and the lights get turned off. It endures when relationships crumble and storms destroy what you've built. It's the one thing that can't be repossessed, stolen, or lost, unless you voluntarily surrender it.

Yet you've been taught to surrender it constantly. You've heard phrases like, *"You can't eat dignity"* or *"You can't pay bills with self-respect,"* and these seemingly practical statements have drained your life of everything good. They sound reasonable, but they're poison disguised as wisdom. They teach you that honor is optional when survival is at stake.

This is a lie that keeps you small. Dignity isn't something you can afford to lose; it's something you can't afford to live without. When you maintain your self-respect through difficult times, you preserve the very foundation that enables you to rebuild. When you trade your dignity for temporary relief, you lose the inner strength needed to create lasting solutions.

Forgive your past. Protect your dignity. These aren't separate practices; they are connected acts of self-preservation that keep your spirit alive even when your circumstances are challenging.

The Internal Fire

Most people never consider the connection between self-respect and the mind itself. Self-respect is often confused with material success. People believe they demonstrate self-respect through the clothes they wear, the home they live in, or the car they drive. But these external markers have nothing to do with genuine self-respect.

True self-respect is an internal fire that no one else can feel, but everyone can see. It's the quiet dignity that shows up in how you speak to yourself, how you set boundaries with others, and how you respond when life tests your character. It's evident in the standards you maintain even when no one is watching.

This internal fire is essential to taking control of your mind and living with sustained motivation. When you truly respect yourself, you stop accepting thoughts and circumstances that diminish you. You refuse to let your mind run wild with self-defeating patterns because you know you deserve better. Self-respect becomes the gatekeeper that determines what you allow into your mental space.

Without this foundation, motivation becomes dependent on external validation and temporary circumstances. With it, motivation flows from an unshakable sense that you are worth the effort, worth the discipline, and worth the patient work of becoming who you're meant to be.

Your Brain Can Change

Neuroplasticity is one of the most encouraging discoveries in modern neuroscience. It's the brain's ability to reorganize itself throughout your life, creating new neural connections, strengthening existing ones, and even forming new pathways for information to travel.

This means the mental patterns that feel permanent aren't actually fixed. The thoughts that seem automatic, the reactions that feel hardwired, the limitations that seem unchangeable can all be transformed through intentional practice and repetition.

Here's what this means practically: every time you choose to think differently, respond differently, or act differently than your usual patterns, you're literally rewiring your brain. When you consistently choose courage over fear, gratitude over complaint, or action over procrastination, you're strengthening those neural pathways and making those responses more natural over time.

The brain that learned to expect disappointment can learn to expect possibility. The mind that developed habits of self-doubt can develop habits of self-confidence. The neural networks that create anxiety and limitation can be replaced with networks that generate calm and capability.

This isn't positive thinking or wishful hoping. It's biological reality. Your brain is designed to adapt based on what you consistently feed it through your thoughts, experiences, and actions. The question isn't whether change is possible, science has proven it is. The question is whether you're willing to do the consistent mental work required to create that change.

Recovery is possible not just from obvious trauma, but from the subtle mental conditioning that keeps you operating below your potential. Your brain has been shaped by years of experience, but it can be reshaped by intentional practice starting today.

The neuroplasticity is already there. The capacity for transformation already exists within you. What's needed now is the faith to begin the process and the discipline to sustain it until new patterns become your new normal.

Planting New Gardens

Change your desires, and you change your life. Most people remain trapped in cycles of pain because they refuse to release the desires that originally enslaved them. They keep watering dead gardens, tending to relationships and dreams that were never meant to flourish, grieving over connections that brought more suffering than joy.

But you can change your field entirely. You can choose to plant new seeds in soil that's actually fertile.

This transformation begins with recognizing where you've been investing your mental energy unwisely. Many people suffer from persistent low self-worth because they tied their sense of value to people who never had the capacity to appreciate them. They mistake intensity for love, drama for passion, and intermittent attention for devotion.

Most heartbreaks aren't tragedies of love lost; they're revelations that genuine love was never present to begin with. True love isn't proven in moments of passion or convenience. It's demonstrated through consistent sacrifice, reliable protection, and unwavering commitment over time.

The person who abandoned you, mistreated you, or failed to see your worth? Strip away the fantasy you built around them, and you'll discover an uncomfortable truth: they never earned access to your heart in the first place. They couldn't honor what they couldn't even recognize. Their inability to value you says nothing about your worth and everything about their blindness.

This is why changing your desires becomes essential. When you stop craving validation from people incapable of giving it, when you stop pursuing relationships built on fear and scarcity, you create space for connections rooted in mutual respect and genuine appreciation.

Love built on fear, "*I'll hurt you before you hurt me*" or "*I'll love less so you can't disappoint me*," isn't love at all. It's emotional self-defense disguised as intimacy. Real love requires the courage to plant seeds in good soil and tend them patiently, rather than desperately trying to grow flowers in barren ground.

Change what you desire, and you change what you attract. Plant your emotional energy in fertile ground, and watch authentic love finally have room to grow. This can only occur in the mind; the body will leave you trapped in this deadly cycle.

The Wounds That Follow

I use relationship examples because they represent some of the most devastating experiences in human life. For many people, relational trauma creates wounds that never fully heal. Most never truly recover from deep heartbreak. They carry the pain silently into their work, their friendships, and their future attempts at love. It reshapes how they see themselves and what they believe they deserve, often without them realizing the connection.

These kinds of wounds don't simply fade with time. They follow you, influencing every decision, every boundary, and every moment of vulnerability that comes afterward.

We've significantly underestimated the psychological and spiritual damage that broken intimate relationships can cause. Our culture treats physical and emotional intimacy as casual entertainment, promoting it in every movie, song, and advertisement as consequence-free pleasure. Yet, when these connections break, trust is shattered, vulnerability is weaponized, and sacred moments become sources of shame.

We're told to *"get over it"* and *"move on"* as if profound intimacy can be discarded without leaving marks on the soul.

This contradiction is damaging and dishonest. We can't simultaneously promote intimacy as meaningless and then expect people to emerge unscathed when those connections are severed or violated. The very depth that makes intimate relationships so potentially healing also makes them devastating when they go wrong.

The truth is, intimate connections, whether physical, emotional, or spiritual, create bonds that aren't easily broken. When those bonds are damaged through betrayal, abandonment, or abuse, the resulting trauma doesn't stay contained in one area of life. It spreads, affecting self-worth, trust, and the ability to be vulnerable in healthy ways.

Understanding this isn't about becoming fearful of intimacy. It's about approaching it with the respect and care it deserves, recognizing that what we do in our closest relationships has the power to heal or wound at the deepest levels. Only when we acknowledge this reality can we begin to make choices that honor both our own hearts and the hearts of others.

LOVE THE MIND, PEACE

Chapter Two
Stillness: The Power Move of the Strong

- *"Be still, and know that I am God."* (Psalm 46:10, KJV)
- Modern society's obsession with busyness
- Studies show that stillness improves productivity and mental health
- **Challenge:** Choose quietness over chaos

The Power of Stillness

The world screams, *"Move faster! Hustle harder!"* Everywhere you turn, someone is telling you that rest is for the weak, that your value is measured by exhaustion and constant motion. But wisdom doesn't shout over the chaos; it whispers, *"Be still."*

Stillness is not the absence of action, it is the presence of intention. The noise pulls you outward into reaction and distraction. True insight pulls you inward toward clarity and purpose.

Real productivity isn't about grinding until you break. It's about aligning your spirit and mind so deeply that your next step feels inevitable rather than frantic. Wisdom doesn't rush; it moves with deliberate clarity. When you slow down enough to listen to your deeper intelligence, you stop chasing what was never meant for you. You stop reacting to every stimulus and start responding from a place of centered awareness.

Modern neuroscience confirms what contemplatives have always known: stillness physically rewires the brain. It lowers stress hormones, strengthens the prefrontal cortex responsible for decision-making, and rebuilds your capacity for sustained focus. You don't need another sleepless night of grinding. You need an hour of clear, intentional stillness. Your stress response can be retrained. Your mind can learn to rest without collapsing into numbness.

Slowing down isn't weakness, it's strategy. In a world running on empty, choosing rest becomes an act of rebellion against systems that profit from your exhaustion. Peace becomes your power source rather than your reward for completing endless tasks.

This kind of stillness is actually a form of strength, not the kind you exert through force, but the kind you access through alignment. When you're genuinely still, you can finally hear the deeper intelligence that has always been guiding you. And when you learn to move from that place of inner knowing, you accomplish more with less effort, create more with less strain, and find solutions that eluded you during all those hours of frantic activity.

Authentic Dreams vs. Borrowed Desires

There's a crucial difference between moving with purpose and rushing from panic. You might feel excitement, yes. You might move with focused energy. But rushing, that frantic, breathless chase, is different. That's anxiety disguised as ambition. When you're hustling without inner peace, even your victories feel hollow. Success built on chaos has no foundation and eventually collapses under its own weight.

Here's how to recognize the difference: authentic dreams don't require constant external validation to feel real. They don't need social media applause or other people's approval to sustain your motivation. These dreams emerge from your deepest values and naturally serve something larger than your immediate comfort.

Borrowed desires, on the other hand, are goals you've absorbed from culture, advertising, or social pressure. If your ultimate dream is to own luxury items primarily to impress others or prove your worth, these aspirations likely came from external programming rather than internal calling. There's nothing inherently wrong with enjoying nice things, but when material accumulation becomes your primary purpose, you've traded authentic fulfillment for social acceptance.

The world will applaud borrowed dreams because they're familiar and non-threatening. But your soul remains quiet because it knows the difference between what you actually want and what you think you should want.

Following your authentic dreams is deeply spiritual, but it isn't religious or ceremonial. These dreams don't need interpreters, gurus, or elaborate rituals. They need clarity, patience, and the courage to distinguish between your voice and the world's noise.

When you encounter people flaunting wealth as wisdom or selling success formulas, step back and protect your mental space. Ask your deeper intelligence, whatever you call that inner knowing, to guide you toward genuine wisdom rather than sophisticated marketing.

Superficial desires don't disappear easily. They fight to maintain their hold on your attention because they've been reinforced by years of cultural messaging. But when you consistently choose clarity over chaos, and purpose over approval, these borrowed dreams eventually lose their power over you. What remains is what truly matters: the authentic vision that has been patiently waiting for you to stop chasing shadows and start building something real.

The Voices That Drive Us

No one rushes to do chores unless there's a reward waiting or a consequence looming Money, praise, freedom, or fear, something external has to be attached to make the task feel worth doing. That's exactly what personal growth feels like for most people in our modern world: not joy, not purpose, just another chore to survive. And if that's how you see self-improvement, you'll avoid it every chance you get.

This happens because we unconsciously adopt one of three motivational "parents" that drive our behavior, each carrying the emotional patterns we learned in childhood.

The **Drill Sergeant Parent** operates through pressure and fear. This voice pushes you with rigid demands, harsh criticism, and the constant threat that you're not doing enough. Growth becomes a military operation where rest is weakness and gentleness is failure. You achieve things, but you're exhausted and never satisfied because the standard keeps rising.

The **Bribing Parent** operates through rewards and external validation. This voice promises treats for good behavior, social media likes for your progress posts, praise for your achievements, and external recognition for your efforts. You become addicted to the applause, but when the rewards disappear, so does your motivation.

The **Crowd Parent** is the loudest and most dangerous. This voice comes from the opinions of people who don't know your story, your struggles, or your true calling, yet feel entitled to judge your choices. You exhaust yourself trying to satisfy strangers on the internet, family members who never took their own risks, or friends who are projecting their fears onto your dreams.

The goal isn't to find the "right" external parent, it's to mature beyond needing any of them. True motivation comes from a different source entirely: your authentic self connected to genuine purpose. This internal guidance doesn't scream with urgency or bribe with rewards. It speaks with quiet clarity about what matters most to you.

When you learn to operate from this internal authority, something beautiful happens: chores become choices, discipline becomes self-respect, and growth becomes an expression of freedom rather than a response to pressure.

The question isn't whether you're motivated. The question is: **which voice are you letting motivate you?** Choose wisely, because that choice determines not just what you accomplish, but who you become in the process.

The Internal Authority

There is a fourth option beyond the three problematic motivational patterns: developing your own internal authority. This isn't another external parent, it's the mature part of yourself that combines wisdom, compassion, and healthy standards.

Your internal authority operates like the best kind of parent you could have had: firm but loving, demanding but fair. It doesn't let you avoid responsibility, but it doesn't crush you with impossible expectations either. It says, *"You live in this life, so you contribute to making it better. Period."* But it balances that demand with genuine care for your well-being.

This internal voice teaches foundational truths about adulthood: you have a responsibility to contribute to your environment and relationships, regardless of your mood or circumstances. You're not the center of the universe, but you're not insignificant either. You share this world, so you share the effort required to improve it.

Unlike the drill sergeant, this authority doesn't operate from fear. Unlike the bribing parent, it doesn't require external rewards. Unlike the crowd, it doesn't change based on popular opinion. It operates from consistent internal values that you've chosen and refined over time.

This authority builds empathy by requiring you to consider how your actions affect others. It develops awareness by making you conscious of your impact on your environment. It creates genuine discipline, not through punishment or rewards, but through consistent alignment with what you know is right.

The difference is crucial: external parents create dependency on their approval, pressure, or rewards. Internal authority creates self-generating motivation. You stop waiting for someone else to push you, bribe you, or validate you. You become your own source of both standards and compassion.

When you develop this internal authority, something powerful happens: you stop needing motivation from outside sources because you've become a source of motivation yourself. You don't need someone else to tell you what matters, you know. You don't need external pressure to act, you're moved by internal purpose.

This is what emotional and spiritual maturity looks like: the ability to parent yourself with both love and accountability, creating the conditions for authentic growth that doesn't depend on anyone else's energy or approval.

Peace, Be Still

The sea was not created to rage endlessly; it was created to carry vessels safely to their destinations. The wind was not made to destroy; it was made to power movement and bring change. When these forces of nature become chaotic, they abandon their true purpose and become obstacles rather than allies.

The same principle applies to the storms within you. Your emotions were not designed to overwhelm and paralyze you; they were meant to provide energy and information for wise action. Your thoughts were not created to spiral into anxiety and doubt; they were designed to process information and generate solutions. When your inner world becomes chaotic, it abandons its purpose of serving your highest good.

This is why you must learn to speak peace over your internal storms. Say to yourself, *"Peace, be still,"* not as a desperate plea, but as a calm command. You are not begging the chaos to end; you are authoritatively redirecting it back

54

to its proper function. Peace is not passive submission, it is strategic power that restores your ability to think clearly, see accurately, and move purposefully.

You must become an ally to your own destiny. A stormy mind cannot carry vision. A chaotic heart cannot hold steady purpose. But when you choose stillness, when you consciously speak peace over your internal world, you allow the turbulent waters inside you to settle, and your deeper wisdom becomes audible again.

Without cooperation from your inner world, your goals will drown in emotional chaos. Storms serve no constructive purpose for your dreams. Peace does. And this stillness is not weakness or avoidance, it is the strategic cultivation of the mental and emotional conditions necessary for clear action.

Stillness gives you back control over your responses. Peace brings your life back on course toward what truly matters. The goal is not to eliminate your emotions or escape from challenging circumstances. The goal is to calm your internal environment so you can use your emotional energy constructively and navigate external challenges from a place of centered strength.

When you master this internal peace, you don't retreat from the world; you engage with it from a position of unshakeable stability, able to lead and contribute rather than simply react and survive.

You are the sea. You are the wind. And when you are at peace, your life becomes navigable again. You become the vessel that carries purpose forward, not the chaos that crashes against your own goals. Your dreams don't need more energy; they need more clarity.

When inner peace prevails, everything else follows naturally. Creativity returns like a rising tide. New ideas surface effortlessly. Motivation bubbles up from deep places you thought had run dry. Direction becomes obvious rather than overwhelming. This is why chaos fights so hard for control of your inner world, because without peace, even your clearest purposes feel unreachable.

So take back control. Speak to your internal storm with the same authority you'd use to quiet a disruption in your own home. You don't need permission to create peace in your own mind. You don't earn tranquility by completing endless tasks or solving every problem first. Peace is declared when you finally decide that inner noise will no longer dictate your choices.

Your real power begins in your silence. That's where your clarity returns. That's where vision becomes possible again. You cannot catch breakthrough insights in the middle of mental chaos, but you absolutely can catch them in cultivated stillness.

Let your inner world mirror the calm that comes after conscious choice. Let the rushing thoughts settle. Let the doubt grow quiet. Let external pressures lose their grip on your internal state. When you become genuinely still, direction appears naturally. The miracle isn't just that internal storms can be calmed, it's that you can finally think clearly again. Peace doesn't make life perfect, but it makes a purposeful life possible.

Here's the crucial difference: storms can only be endured, but stillness can be utilized. Stillness is where real strategy begins. If your life feels chaotic and out of control, examine your inner pace first. Your next breakthrough might be waiting in the quiet space you haven't created yet.

Being still doesn't mean doing nothing. It means engaging with what truly matters without inner noise, without panic, without the pressure that clouds judgment. It's focused action from a centered place. It's clean. It's clear. It's sustainable.

Ideas Are Like Fish

Ideas are like fish; they don't swim toward chaotic waters. If you want to catch insights that will transform your life, you must first still the waters of your mind and create space for them to surface naturally. The same mental environment that feels threatening when turbulent becomes incredibly supportive once peace enters the situation. This shift can happen remarkably quickly when you consciously choose stillness over chaos.

Movement vs. Direction

People often assume that constant movement is the solution to stagnation. But movement without clear direction is just sophisticated chaos. Stillness is what gives purposeful movement its meaning and power. Rest isn't surrender; it's strategic recalibration that allows you to move more effectively when action is needed.

Creating Space for Wisdom

Your deepest wisdom is most often accessed in quietude. If you're not hearing your inner guidance clearly, the problem may not be distance from your authentic self; it may be too much external noise drowning out the signal.

Intentionally creating silence is essential for accessing your clearest thinking.

Stillness vs. Stagnation

Don't confuse deliberate stillness with passive stagnation. Stagnation is an obstacle that prevents growth; stillness is a strategy that enables it. Stillness gives your spirit space to expand and your vision room to develop without the constant pressure of external demands.

The Power of Calm

A genuinely calm mind becomes remarkably powerful because fear-based reactions no longer control it. When you operate from centeredness, you are much harder to manipulate, rush, or trick into accepting less than you deserve. Clarity creates natural boundaries.

Your Internal Anchor

Think of your life as a vessel navigating through storms. External turbulence is inevitable, but you don't have to let it penetrate your inner world. As long as you maintain stillness at your core, external waves lose their power to destabilize you. Inner peace becomes your anchor.

The Radical Act of Pausing

Sometimes, the most powerful thing you can do is pause, not quit, but consciously create space to breathe and trust that meaningful progress can happen even during periods of apparent inactivity. Growth often occurs in the quiet spaces between actions. Let the world operate at its frantic pace. You remain anchored in purposeful calm. Let others shout over each other for attention. You stay centered in your own clarity. When external pressure becomes overwhelming, you have the power to whisper back, "Peace, be still," and create the mental environment where your best ideas can finally surface.

Breaking Free from the Busyness Trap

Modern society worships busyness like a false god. We've been taught that if we run fast enough, grind hard enough, and stay constantly in motion, peace and fulfillment will eventually catch up with us. But this is a fundamental lie. The means could not be more disconnected from the end. If you believe that rushing headfirst into endless activity will somehow lead to satisfaction, you'll wake up one day exhausted, overcommitted, and still feeling empty. Busyness without clear purpose is just noise dressed up as productivity. It looks impressive from the outside but leads nowhere meaningful.

Here's the truth that cuts through the cultural programming: peace cannot be chased; it must be chosen. Fulfillment isn't a destination you arrive at through frantic effort. It's a way of being that emerges when you align your actions with your deepest values and priorities. If you think you're behind in life because you started late, got distracted, or made mistakes, remember this: you are not behind anyone else's timeline. You are exactly where you need to be if you start now with genuine purpose and full presence. Comparison is the enemy of contentment, and there is no cosmic schedule you've fallen behind on.

The wisdom you seek isn't hidden in some distant achievement or future circumstance. It's present and available right now, but it doesn't scream for attention over the cultural noise. It whispers. When you slow down enough to listen to your deeper intelligence, you'll discover that lasting motivation doesn't come from external pressure but from internal alignment with what truly matters to you. This is why choosing quietness over chaos becomes revolutionary. Stillness isn't passivity; it's strategic power. In the calm spaces, you can finally hear your authentic priorities above the noise of everyone else's urgency.

Practically, this means capturing your clearest thoughts when they surface. Write them down. Give them weight. Let these aligned insights guide your day instead of letting external demands and other people's priorities take your schedule hostage. It also means curating your information diet carefully. Limit social media consumption, not because it's inherently evil, but because even good advice becomes overwhelming noise when it's constant. Too much input, even from valuable sources, can drown out your ability to hear your own direction. Choose your influences wisely and let your authentic inner wisdom have the loudest voice in your decision-making. The answers you're seeking are closer than you think.

The Bull in the Arena

Too much of a good thing can indeed turn on you. Ambition, in its proper place, can lift your life. But ambition without wisdom? That's how you get used. That's how you get ridden. The bull is strong. The bull is proud. The bull is ready to fight for its space, and that's exactly why they drag him back into the arena, day after day. The bull that bucks is the bull they use. His resistance makes him a show. His strength becomes a trap.

If the bull stood still and refused to react or buck, they would stop using him. He would be no fun for the crowd. He'd be released, put out to pasture, and left alone. But ambition without wisdom keeps dragging him back into the dirt. The world does the same to you. If you keep bucking, keep moving, keep trying to throw off the pressure without ever being still, you'll find yourself back in the rodeo over and over. They use reactive minds, not calm ones. They don't ride the quiet ones. They don't ride the ones who refuse to play. The ones who stop making noise, who refuse to flinch, fight, or perform, are the ones they eventually leave alone.

We get no reward for the performance, no glory, no trophy, just the illusion of control and a check that disappears the minute it arrives. Paycheck to paycheck is just another version of "room and board." No rest. No wealth. Just survival. So be still. Stop dancing for the crowd. Stop bending just so someone else can mount your back. And don't waste your energy trying to buck them off, because that's what they want. Don't play the game at all. Don't be their entertainment.

Stillness is strength. Calm is rebellion. Refusing to perform for a system that doesn't serve you is wisdom, not weakness. Let them wonder why they can't ride you anymore. They use your energy because they can't generate their own. And they'll keep using it until you learn to go still, not dead still, not passive, but strategic stillness.

The rodeo doesn't care about the bull's bruises. The crowd just wants a show. Your pain becomes their paycheck if you don't step off the stage. Your struggle feeds their system while leaving you exhausted and broken. Strength without wisdom is just stamina for suffering. You don't need to prove your power; you need to protect it. Stop showing it off where it's not valued, where it's only exploited for someone else's gain.

The calm bull lives longer. He breathes easier. He's not famous, but he's free. He doesn't make headlines, but he makes his own choices. Peace is more powerful than pride, and freedom is worth more than applause. You were not created to be someone else's ride. Your ambition wasn't meant to feed the system that exploits it. It was meant to build your own purpose.

The paycheck that vanishes before it hits your account proves you are being ridden, your time, your energy, your life force. And the applause you hear isn't for you; it's for the show your struggle provides. Stillness isn't quitting. It's quitting the performance. It's stepping out of the cycle that keeps you bucking for their entertainment. It's choosing pasture over pressure, peace over proving yourself.

Let them call you lazy. Let them call you soft. But you'll still be standing long after they've burned out from chasing noise and manufactured urgency. When you stop responding to every provocation, you break the game. When you stop fighting back against every slight, they have nothing to ride. That's when your real peace begins. Busyness is their control mechanism. Stillness is your power source. Rest is not a reward you earn after exhaustion, it's a strategic weapon you use to protect your energy. Your value is not measured by how much pressure you can withstand. It's demonstrated by how wisely you choose to move. Don't be ridden by circumstances, expectations, or other people's urgency. Be rooted in your own purpose.

Closing: The Emotion You Control

If you must feel the condition before it happens, and you do, then the peace you seek from wealth must be felt before wealth arrives. This is the design of the mind and the spirit. As the Scripture says, *"Faith is the substance of things hoped for, the evidence of things not seen."* Faith creates the feeling. The feeling attracts the reality. You don't receive peace after success; you build success because you already carry peace.

Practice peace now, not later. Practice it daily through faith in God, stillness, and intentional focus on what He has already done in your life. All things will be added in their proper time, but peace does not wait on circumstances. Peace is not the result of perfect conditions. Peace is a decision you make while the storm is still raging. Peace is a choice before it becomes a reward.

This book is not just about building wealth. Permanent motivation is about building your spirit, your health, your wellness, and your peace. And while you're building those things, why not bring some wealth along for the ride? You're not chasing money, you're chasing meaning. And when you chase meaning, money tends to keep up.

My goal is to permanently motivate you to help you live the life you were always meant to live, not a life defined by things, but a life anchored in purpose. When your life is aligned with helping others, motivation stops being temporary. It becomes a current that never runs dry. Service becomes your superpower. And the truth is, it already lives inside you.

Elevated emotions like joy, excitement, and purpose create a natural high. People spend their entire lives trying to recreate that high through external things. But these emotions were never outside. They live inside you. They begin with you, and they can be reactivated at will. The outside world does not give them to you; it only triggers what was already yours.

The phrase *"like a child on Christmas morning"* did not come from children. It came from adults looking backward. Children don't intellectualize joy, they are joy. Adults remember the excitement they once felt: the anticipation, the electricity in their body. But as life adds burdens, that spark begins to fade.

The toys were never the source of the joy. The child was. The outside world only reflected what was already burning inside. The volcano of excitement did not erupt because of wrapping paper or snowfall. It came from belief, from anticipation, from a pure emotional readiness for joy. The joy came from within.

But for most adults, that volcano has cooled. The magic of Christmas fades. Winter, once thrilling, becomes a burden. The coats feel heavier. Walking becomes cautious. Driving becomes tense. Joy gives way to routine, and the soul forgets what it used to know.

What I am trying to tell you is this: that volcano is still inside you. It never left. It never died. It was buried under years of noise, responsibility, and external focus. But it can erupt again, not through new toys, new cars, or fleeting highs, but through deliberate practice.

You have the power to ignite that energy at any moment. You can tap into emotions that slow aging, sharpen your mind, and rekindle passion. You can take control of what many have already surrendered to circumstances. Most people wait for something to give them a reason. But you can become the reason.

It starts with shutting out the noise. It continues with meditation on truth. It grows with daily connection to God and the belief that your best emotions, peace, excitement, and joy, are still yours to command. These emotions are not rewards. They are tools. You just forgot where you placed them.

This is **Permanent Motivation**. Not a moment. Not a mood. A lifestyle. A choice. A spiritual discipline. And it is available to you now.

Reflection: Reigniting Your Inner Volcano

Take 5 minutes. Be honest. Write your answers in a journal or notebook.

1. When was the last time you felt true excitement or peace before an outcome arrived?
    (Describe the moment. What were you feeling before the "bang" happened?)
2. What outside things have you been crediting for your emotions, money, success, approval, or material things?
    (Write them down so you can take the power back.)
3. How can you practice the emotions of peace, joy, and purpose today, before any circumstances change?
    (Think joy. Think daily.)

4. What does Permanent Motivation look like for you right now?
   (Describe the lifestyle, not just the results.)

Declaration (Say aloud or write):

"My peace and purpose are not controlled by outside forces. I reignite the joy, energy, and motivation within me today. I walk in Permanent Motivation."

Chapter Three
Depression Is Not Your Identity

- *"The LORD is nigh unto them that are of a broken heart."* (Psalm 34:18, KJV)
- Understanding depression as a condition, not your fate.
- Psychological research on hope therapy and self-perception.
- Action steps: Separating "I feel" from "I am."

You are not your pain. You are not your diagnosis. Depression may describe your season, but it doesn't define your soul. Science shows that identity plays a massive role in recovery, and Scripture reminds us that God is close to the brokenhearted. It's time to remove the lies that tried to name you and remember who you really are.

You are more than a title. You are an incredible, wonderfully made being. Before the world gave you a name, a job, or a role, you were already someone. You were already loved. You already carried the image of the great *I AM THAT I AM*.

Move, and move now. Not into busyness. Not into more titles. Move into the daily practice of releasing the pain response from your life. Depression often grows when we stay frozen in place. Looking back clouds every step forward.

Sing aloud to God: **"Every little step I take, we'll be together."**

Reclaim yourself. Put away the false labels. The world may need your job titles, but you don't need them for identity. Use them only when necessary, and only until you can shake them off for good.

If a title defines you, it's not really you. And it's unhealthy. Titles become trinkets of deception when they're confused with identity. Accomplishments can be beautiful, but they should wear only one title: **gratefulness to God**. No other label can hold your worth.

It doesn't matter what the title is: Doctor. Lawyer. Scientist. Professional athlete. Movie star. None of these were ever meant to define the human soul.

In fact, the more tightly you hold onto a title, the more vulnerable you become to depression. Titles can be taken away. Roles can end. But **you remain**. You were never born to be a movie star or an athlete. These are just creative professions sparked by man's imagination.

You were born to be you. Find yourself, and happiness will follow. Seek a title other than *I AM*, and unhappiness will flood in and drown your hope.

When Titles Become Chains

Education is a beautiful thing, as long as it doesn't become your entire identity. It is a tool meant to serve your purpose, not define who you are. Being a doctor is a blessing, but it should never replace your true self. Healing the sick is one of the most sacred callings, and many doctors are genuinely called to do that work.

However, the title *"doctor"* is not the calling. The **act of healing** is. When healers lose sight of who they are at the core, the joy that once fueled their work begins to fade. The responsibility shifts from serving others to carrying the weight of expectation. That's how healthcare has evolved into a system driven by pressure and profit, rather than peace and purpose. The mission has been distorted by the weight of the title, and tons of student loan debt.

This pattern exists far beyond medicine. Doctors need to return to being healers. Teachers must reclaim their roles as nurturers. Lawyers should remember their purpose as defenders of justice, not merely protectors of status.

When the systems of the world begin to value **prestige more than purpose**, identity itself becomes heavy. It stops feeling like a gift and starts feeling like a trap.

Depression doesn't always come from weakness. Often, it comes from **misalignment**. People aren't breaking down because they're incapable. They're breaking down because they were never meant to carry the weight of a false identity. When who you are gets buried beneath who you're expected to be, the soul begins to ache.

Motivational Thoughts

1. You were born for purpose, not for titles. Titles can change. Purpose does not.
2. The world will name you a thousand things. God called you once.
3. Looking back keeps you locked up. Movement forward, even small, unlocks new joy.
4. Your worth was set before your achievements. It cannot be increased or decreased.
5. Depression often begins where identity ends. Reclaim who you are without the labels.
6. Your value is eternal. No career, no failure, no status can erase it.
7. When you seek titles for identity, the world becomes

your judge. Let God be the judge.

8. Even great accomplishments cannot satisfy a soul built for divine purpose.
9. A healer without joy is a doctor with a heavy coat. Shed the weight.
10. Roles serve you. You do not serve roles. Keep the difference clear.
11. The moment you detach from the title, peace returns.
12. Permanent motivation comes when you live as yourself, not as the world's expectations.
13. You are not becoming someone. You are returning to who you've always been.
14. When you stop performing, you start living. That's where freedom begins.

***

Depression Is Not Your Identity

Ask yourself this question: **Why is it so easy to be unhappy?**

The answer begins before you ever drew your first breath. Long before your eyes opened to the light of this world, you were already a master learner, not by choice, but by design. In the womb, you were absorbing the emotional environment around you. You learned without question or hesitation. Whatever emotional patterns surrounded you became familiar. There was no filter, no critical thinking, only absorption.

So, the emotional climate of your earliest environment became your baseline normal. For many people, stress, anxiety, or unhappiness became as familiar as breathing.

These patterns were learned before conscious choice was even possible. That was the beginning of your emotional programming.

But it does **not** have to be the end of your story.

You Have Been Lied To

As you grew, you were taught to accept the world's version of normal. But much of what you learned was not universal truth, it was cultural programming, designed to keep you pursuing things that can never truly satisfy you.

You were trained to agree with systems that don't serve your well-being. You looked at the burdens placed on you by society, family expectations, and economic pressure, and decided to call them simply "life."

"That's just the way things are," you were told.

No. That's the way you've been conditioned to accept things. It is not the way you have to continue. You have the power to examine these inherited beliefs, and choose differently.

The Trap of Competitive Happiness

You were also taught that life is fundamentally competitive. That some people win while others lose. That every accomplishment proves your worth, and every setback reveals your weakness. That happiness comes from rising above others, rather than from inner contentment.

But here's what this mindset creates: People who can only feel good about themselves when others are struggling. Their satisfaction becomes dependent on comparison, rather than genuine fulfillment. They achieve external markers of success but remain internally empty, because their happiness requires other people's failure to sustain it.

This is **not victory**. This is conditional happiness that disappears the moment someone else succeeds, or when you're no longer "ahead" of whoever you're measuring yourself against.

The Truth about Your Emotional Patterns

The depression, anxiety, or persistent unhappiness you may experience is **not** who you are. It's a learned response pattern, one that became so familiar, you began to mistake it for your identity. Just as you learned language, social behaviors, and countless other skills, you also learned emotional patterns from your earliest environment.

The difference is that no one taught you emotional patterns can be **unlearned** and replaced with healthier ones. You can develop new neural pathways, new responses to stress, and new ways of interpreting life's challenges. Your emotional baseline can be reset, but it requires the same kind of intentional practice you would use to learn any new skill.

Depression may be something you're **experiencing**, but it is not something you **are**. Recognizing that difference is the first step toward freedom.

Failure Does Not Exist

Most people believe they fear failure. But they don't, because failure isn't what they think it is.

What we call **failure** is simply information. It's

feedback about what didn't work under specific circumstances at a particular time. It's data about a strategy, an approach, or a decision on timing. But it is not a verdict about your worth, your potential, or your future.

When something doesn't work out as planned, you haven't failed. You've discovered one way that doesn't work in those specific conditions.

Thomas Edison didn't fail 1,000 times before inventing the light bulb. He found 1,000 ways that didn't work, which brought him closer to the one that did.

The Choice Point

What people actually fear isn't failure. It's the **choice point** that comes after disappointment.

When something doesn't work out, you reach a crossroads. You can either use the information you've gained to adjust your approach, or you can interpret the experience as proof that you should stop trying.

The fear isn't about the outcome not matching your expectations. The fear is about what you'll choose to believe about yourself **when that happens**

If you choose to stop pursuing something after a setback, you haven't failed. You've made a conscious decision based on new insight about your priorities, your circumstances, or your goals.

Maybe you discovered the goal wasn't truly important to you. Maybe you realized your energy would be better invested elsewhere.

Maybe external circumstances changed your available options.

These are all **valid reasons** to redirect your path. They are not failures. They are **course corrections**.

The Ongoing Journey

Every pursuit teaches you something, whether it ends in the outcome you originally wanted or not. Every attempt builds skills, reveals preferences, creates connections, or clarifies what you truly want versus what you only thought you wanted.

The journey continues until **you** decide it's complete.

Sometimes, completion looks like achieving your original goal. Sometimes, it looks like discovering a better one along the way. Sometimes, it looks like learning what you don't want and redirecting your energy toward what you do.

Practical Application

When something doesn't work out as planned, ask yourself better questions:

- What did I learn that I can apply next time?
- What worked well that I should keep doing?
- What assumptions need to be adjusted?
- Is this goal still aligned with what I actually want?
- What would I do differently with the information I have now?

These questions turn disappointment into **education**, and setbacks into **strategy sessions**.

That's not failure. That's how growth actually works.

The Two Deadly Vehicles of the Rat Race

The second reason we're so good at being sad is because the **outside world trains us to be**. It reinforces these emotions. It recruits us into the **rat race** before we even understand what a race is.

And the rat race comes fully equipped. It offers vehicles of unhappiness, lined up and waiting for you to take the wheel. They promise **speed**, **success**, and **significance**, but deliver **exhaustion**, **anxiety**, and **quiet despair**.

I will focus on the two biggest and most dangerous cars in this race: **The Beauty Car** and **The Money Car**.

These are the luxury traps that steal joy and drive millions into a life of comparison, pressure, and burnout.

The Beauty Car: Where the Race Begins

The Beauty Car arrives early in life, usually in school. For many, it begins as early as first grade, an age when no child should be competing for worth or identity.

School is the first time most children encounter a crowd beyond their family. And what do they have to offer? A smile. A simple conversation about cartoons or songs.

At that age, there's no concept of money. No ambition. No materialism. Only **presence**.

But the world wastes no time. It teaches its first cruel lesson quickly: You are judged by how "cute" you are.

That becomes the **unspoken currency** of value.

Attention is given not based on spirit or soul, but on surface.

This is where the unholy battle for approval begins.

The so-called "cute" kids receive the praise, the smiles, the attention. The rest are left out in the cold, watching, learning, absorbing a painful, false truth: **My value depends on how they see me.**

The Beauty Car takes off fast. Most of us are left behind in the dust.

This is where many first begin to hate themselves, not because they were born broken, but because they were told, with words or silence, that they didn't qualify for love, attention, or acceptance.

Worse still, those labeled "cute" learn they are driving the fastest car. They begin to believe worth is something you wear on your face, not something you live through your heart. Appearance replaces kindness. Looks overshadow character. And creativity is forgotten.

This is how the **silent birth of depression** begins, not in adulthood, not even in the teenage years, but in **first grade**.

That is the true tragedy. And it is something few adults ever talk about.

They remember the cruelty of children. But they forget the truth that matters most: **Those wounds still bleed beneath grown-up skin.**

They were never properly healed.

"Kids can be cruel."

That is the understatement of the century.

To Every Child Who Looked in the Mirror

To every child who went home after school, stood in front of the mirror, and stared at a "hideous creature" they had been introduced to by cruelty: **I see you. I am with you. I love you.**

> *You were lied to.*
> *Your worth was never based on their words.*
> *Your value was not up for vote.*
> *And it still isn't.*
>
> *What they said or didn't say...*
> *What they praised or ignored...*
> *What they mocked or admired...*
>
> **Had nothing to do with the truth of who you are.**
>
> *You are **still here**.*
> *You are **still worthy**.*
> *And you **always were**.*

***

The Beauty-Car: A Wreck You Can Walk Away From

The beauty-car that the rat race forces us to drive does not retire in childhood. It follows us. It shifts gears. It speeds up. And as we grow, the outside world continues to reinforce the pressure to stay behind the wheel.

Songs, movies, advertisements, television, and social media all keep the race alive.

They scream what beauty should *look like.*

They tell you what to buy.
They define what face and body you should wear.
They even suggest who you should love.

The Money Car: When the Race Accelerates

As we grow older, the second car pulls up. It is the **Money Car**.

By the teenage years, and certainly by adulthood, beauty alone no longer wins races. Now, money becomes the measure: the clothes you wear, the phone you carry, the neighborhood you live in.

Just like in childhood, the fastest drivers rise to the front. The rich, the privileged, the ones who flaunt it all race ahead while the rest try to catch up, or eventually give up.

But here is the truth the race will never tell you: **You were never meant to drive these cars.**

None of it has ever been true about you.
You are not their opinions.
You are not the false standards they created.
And you do not have to keep living beneath the wreckage of these cars.

***

The Freedom of the Unconcerned

You often hear people say,

"Old folks don't give a damn anymore."
"Look at the way he combs his hair."
"Look at the clothes she's wearing."

As if caring less is a sign of defeat.
It's not.
It's a sign of freedom.

I remember sitting in my car one day, watching an elderly man cross the street. His pants were high-waters, nearly up to his knees. His shoes, maybe worth twenty dollars. His shirt was half tucked in, half hanging out. There was no fashion statement. No effort to impress. Just freedom.

The part of town made it clear he wasn't struggling financially. If anything, he was probably wealthy, or at least had access to wealth. He walked like a man who had made peace with himself a long time ago.

At his age, he had no one to impress.
No social approval to chase.
He didn't care what women thought of him.
And he certainly didn't care what other men thought either.

That man was free.

And that freedom made him look better than any brand-name suit or luxury cologne ever could.

14 Motivational Sentences

1. The beauty-car only wins if you agree to keep driving it.
2. Media profits from your insecurity. They sell it. You buy it. Stop purchasing lies.
3. Their opinions were never facts, they were fears projected outward.
4. The elderly man's clothes were not a sign of poverty.

They were a sign of peace.

5. Wealth isn't found in approval. It's found in the absence of needing approval.

6. You were not created to be decoration. You were created to be divine.

7. Every right thought is wisdom. Every wise decision is freedom.

8. The race was rigged from the start. The only way to win is to leave it.

9. The mirror or the market does not validate your worth.

10. Freedom arrives when opinions lose their power to shape you.

11. The elderly are not careless. They are clear about what matters.

12. Permanent motivation means living for purpose, not popularity.

13. The beauty-car crashes every driver eventually. Step out while you can.

14. Your value doesn't retire. It reveals itself when the race ends.

◢ Reflection: Step Out of the Beauty-Car

Before you move forward, take a few quiet moments to answer these questions. Be honest. Be raw. This is for you.

1. Whose definition of beauty have you been trying to meet?

Was it someone from your past?

A parent? A partner? Social media?

What image have you been chasing, and does it belong to you?

2. What messages have shaped how you see your body, your face, your worth?

List three you've heard or felt (e.g., *"I'm not attractive unless…"* or *"I need to look younger to matter."*)

3. What did that race cost you?

Be specific: Energy? Joy? Relationships? Confidence?

4. What would it look like to step out of that car today?

No more chasing. No more proving. Just being.

Write one sentence declaring your freedom.

Example: "I do not belong to their standards. I belong to truth."

5. Speak truth over yourself.

Write 2–3 affirming statements in your own words that are true and yours, not borrowed from the world.

Example:

- "I am not behind. I am not broken. I am more than enough."
- "My worth doesn't need proof. I was created worthy."

⬢ Reminder: You are not what they sold you.

- *You are not what they liked or scrolled past.*
- *You are not what you wore, weighed, or posted.*
- *You are **you**, and that's already **sacred**.*

Chapter Four
The Spirit of Motivation: Praying Without Ceasing

- *"Pray without ceasing."* (1 Thessalonians 5:17, KJV)
- How continuous prayer strengthens neural pathways of hope
- Studies linking gratitude, prayer, and brain health
- **Strategy**: Building prayer into your daily rhythm

Prayer isn't a lifeline you throw in emergencies. It's oxygen for your soul. Neuroscience shows that regular prayer changes your brain's wiring, making you more resilient, hopeful, and connected. God commands us to pray without ceasing because He knows the human spirit needs constant contact with the Source. Prayer isn't your last resort. It's your first strategy.

The Mind Overrides the Body without You Even Knowing It

The Power of Expectation

Let's talk about something most people never stop to consider.

According to research, it can take anywhere from **10 to 120 minutes** for your body to fully absorb and use water. This depends on factors like what you've eaten, how hydrated you already are, and your individual biology.

So here's the question that changes everything:

If it takes that long for water to actually enter your bloodstream, why does the feeling of thirst disappear almost instantly after just a few sips?

The answer reveals something profound about how you're designed. Your **mind** responds to **expectation** faster than your **body** responds to physical change. The moment you begin drinking, your brain sends the signal to stop feeling thirsty. No cells have been nourished yet. No organs have received hydration. The bloodstream is still waiting.

But your mind already believes help is on the way, and that belief is powerful enough to override immediate physical reality.

Relief Is a Decision Before It's a Condition

This isn't just about water. This is about how your entire system works.

Relief often comes from the decision to **trust the process**, not from waiting for complete proof that the process has worked. Your brain tells your body to calm down based on expectation, not evidence.

If your **subconscious** can automatically override physical sensations based on belief, what could your **conscious spirit** do with intentional faith?

This is where the deeper power lies.

The Spiritual Dimension

Spiritual connection rewires physical reaction. When you're connected to something larger than immediate circumstances, your spirit can tell your body: "We're already being taken care of" **even before** external conditions change.

Prayer and faith quiet internal panic faster than physical proof ever could.

The calm doesn't come from seeing the solution. It comes from **trusting** that the solution is already in motion.

This isn't wishful thinking. It's recognizing that you were designed with an override system that **responds to faith**. Just as your body stops signaling thirst before hydration reaches your cells, your spirit can experience peace **before** circumstances align with your hopes.

Practical Application

Permanent motivation works the same way.

You don't wait until you **feel** motivated to act. You act based on **faith** that motivation will follow action.

You don't wait until fear disappears to move forward. You move forward trusting that **courage** will meet you in the movement.

Your transformation doesn't have to wait for perfect conditions.
You only need to believe that what you need is **already moving toward you**.

When you speak **peace** over anxiety, **strength** over weakness, or **hope** over despair, you're activating the same override system that quiets thirst before the water reaches your bloodstream.

Faith speaks **before** the facts.

Your body and circumstances will follow what your spirit accepts as true.

This is not fantasy. This is how you were designed to operate: **Belief first. Evidence second.**

What This Means for Motivation and Prayer

If your **mind** can calm your **body** by faith, not by the result, then your **spirit** can do even more when aligned with **God**.

This is what it means to **pray without ceasing**.

It's not just about constant words.

It's about staying in a state of **awareness**, **alignment**, and **trust** that tells your mind and body: "We're covered. Help is already on the way."

Motivation isn't about pumping yourself up.

It's about training your inner system to respond to **belief**, not **burnout**.

Just like thirst, exhaustion is often a **signal**.

But faith can **quiet the chaos** even before the full result arrives.

When Thoughts Don't Feel Like Yours

I used to wonder, and maybe you have too: Why do so many thoughts pop into my mind without permission?

Not just random ideas, but things I never wanted to think about. Sometimes they're dark. Sometimes they're pointless. Other times, they're distractions that show up at the worst possible moments.

And then there are the songs. Catchy ones. Annoying ones. Songs I like, and songs I hate. They loop in my head like a broken record. Over and over. Loud, persistent, and completely uninvited.

I've sat in silence and asked myself: "Why is this in my head right now?"

"Why can't I get it to stop?"

These thoughts don't feel like my thoughts. They feel like **intrusions**. Like static interrupting a clear broadcast.

Here's what I discovered:

Your mind is incredibly powerful, but it's also constantly **programmable**.

It absorbs far more than you realize from everything around you.

What you **see**, **hear**, and **experience** begins to echo in your mental space, not because you **chose** it, but simply because you were **present** when it happened.

Your mind doesn't distinguish between what you focus on intentionally and what crosses your awareness accidentally. It records everything and plays it back at random, often when you least expect, or want, it.

This is why taking control of your **mental input** becomes so crucial.

Unless you're intentional about what you allow into your mind, the noise will continue.

The random thoughts, the unwanted songs, the intrusive ideas, they'll keep playing on repeat, because your mind is simply doing what it was designed to do: **process and replay** everything it encounters.

The question isn't why these thoughts appear.

The question is: **What are you going to do about the programming?**

Taking Back Authority through Prayer

This is why **praying without ceasing** is not just a spiritual practice. It's a **mental defense strategy**.

When you pray consistently, not only in crisis but as a rhythm of life, you begin to **reclaim your mental space**.

*Prayers **replace noise with stillness**.*
They shift distraction into direction.
They transform randomness into order.
*They **ground** you when your thoughts feel scattered and foreign.*

You do not fight evil thoughts with more thoughts.
*You fight them with **truth**.*
*You fight them with **stillness**.*
*You fight them with **presence**.*

Prayer isn't about fixing everything instantly.
*It's about **refusing to give chaos the final word**.*

***

The moment you realize you are **not your thoughts**, you become free.

You gain the authority to decide what stays and what leaves.

That is where **mental freedom** begins.

And that is how spiritual practice becomes **mental mastery**.

When People Give Up on Their Minds

Most people, whether they realize it or not, have given up on their minds.

Not because they are weak.
Not because they are lazy.
*But because they've been conditioned to believe there is **no real hope** for mental control.*

So they start to live as if their **mind has a mind of its own**.

Thoughts run wild. Distractions take over.
*Negative ideas begin to dictate how they feel **before they even get out of bed**.*

Each day becomes a **battle lost before the fight even begins**.

The mind sets the emotional tone, not based on truth or purpose, but on whatever noise was loudest the night before: yesterday's stress, last week's worry, or random anxieties that have **nothing to do with today**.

Instead of rising up to reclaim their mental space, many simply **surrender to the chaos**.

They stop believing change is possible.
They accept mental disorder as normal.
They resign themselves to being victims of their own

thoughts.

*But it **is** possible to regain control.*
*The mind can be **trained.***
*It can be **renewed.***
*Mental patterns can be **interrupted and replaced** with healthier ones.*

It all starts with believing you still have the power to choose what gets **attention** in your mind and what gets **ignored**.

That choice is always available, **even when it doesn't feel like it**.

Especially when it doesn't feel like it.

The Morning Anxiety Loop

Old Pattern: Wake up and immediately start worrying about the day ahead. Mentally rehearse everything that could go wrong. Feel overwhelmed before even getting out of bed.

Interruption: As soon as you notice the worry spiral starting, **physically sit up** and take **three deep breaths**. This breaks the mental momentum.

Replacement: Ask yourself three specific questions:

- "What is one thing I'm looking forward to today?"
- "What is one thing I can control right now?"
- "What am I grateful for in this moment?"

This practice redirects your mind toward **possibility** and **presence** instead of fear.

The Comparison Trap on Social Media

Old Pattern: Scrolling through social media and automatically comparing your behind-the-scenes reality to everyone else's highlight reel, leading to feelings of inadequacy or jealousy.

Interruption: The moment you notice the comparison starting, pause and close the app immediately. Don't try to think your way out of it while still looking at the triggering content.

Replacement: Open your notes app and write down three specific things you've accomplished recently, or three qualities you appreciate about your own life. This shifts focus from external comparison to internal appreciation.

The Catastrophic Thinking Spiral

Old Pattern: When something goes wrong, immediately jumping to worst-case scenarios.

One mistake becomes, *"I always mess up."*
One rejection becomes, *"I'll never succeed."*
One conflict becomes, *"This relationship is doomed."*

Interruption: Notice the words *"always," "never," "everything,"* or *"nothing"* in your thoughts, these are red flags for catastrophic thinking.

Stop and ask: *"Is this thought helping me solve the problem or just making me feel worse?"*

Replacement: Reframe using specific, time-limited language: *"This particular situation didn't work out,"* instead of, *"I always fail."*

Then ask: *"What's one small step I can take to improve this situation?"*

This moves you from helpless victim to active problem-solver.

The key is that the **interruption must happen before the pattern gains momentum**, and the **replacement must be specific and practiced**, not just "think positive thoughts."

Who's actually in Control?

We've handed over control of our minds to almost everything:

- ⌨ Devices
- 🧠 Trauma
- 🖥 Media
- 💬 Public opinion
- 💀 And yes, spiritual enemies

We've been told, either directly or subtly:

"This is just how it is."
"That's just the devil."
"Ignore him and do your best."

But that's not how Christ moved.
He didn't ignore the enemy.
He silenced him.
He cast him out.
He declared, "It is written."

He took back mental and spiritual authority, **and left us the blueprint**.

Your Mind Was Never Meant to Be on Autopilot

Your mind is not a loose cannon. It is not a lost cause. It is a **temple**. A **command center**. A **battlefield** where you are called to win, **every single day**.

The spirit of motivation does not thrive in chaos. It flows through **control**, **alignment**, and **truth**. It does not arrive through noise or panic. It arrives when your inner world is in sync with your higher calling.

You are not powerless.
*You are **powerful** when you are **aligned**.*
*You are **steady** when you are **centered**.*
*And **praying without ceasing** is the rhythm that keeps you in that power.*

It is the **heartbeat of a life rooted in purpose**.

How to Replace Thoughts That Don't Belong

When a thought enters that does not align with your peace, **replace it**.

Do not argue with it. Do not wrestle with it. Do not give it a stage.

Speak truth over it.

Truth doesn't need to raise its voice to be effective.

Just say what is real. Say what is grounded. Say what aligns with your purpose.

Use **breath work** to anchor your spirit. Inhale slowly. Hold. Exhale even slower. Let your body remember that it is **safe**. Let your breath remind your mind that it is not in charge.

This is how you **train stillness to live inside you**.

Speak **affirmations** that come from truth, not trends. Say: "I am aligned. I am present. I am guided. I am protected."

Do not wait for the feeling to match the words. **The words reshape the feeling. Repetition reshapes the mind.**

Use **scripture** as both weapon and shield. Find one verse that aligns with what you need and carry it throughout your day. Say it when the thought comes. Say it when your peace feels shaky.

You are not just speaking words.

You are **reclaiming territory**.

You Can't Just Pretend the Chaos Isn't There

Ignoring the chaos in your mind is part of the process, but it is **not** the final step.

You cannot build a new life by pretending the old one doesn't exist.

You do not defeat darkness by closing your eyes.

You defeat it by **turning on the light**.

Yes, ignoring thoughts that don't serve you is wise. But that's only **one** part of the strategy.

Real transformation, real **spiritual discipline**, happens when you take full responsibility for what stays and what goes.

The Rhythm of Mental Renewal

(Not a formula, but a framework that brings peace.)

1. Prepare

Expect the noise. Don't be shocked when fear shows up. Don't be thrown off when distractions arrive. They are part of the process. Anticipate them, so they lose their power.

2. Ignore

Do not feed thoughts that drain your energy or focus. Don't wrestle with them. Don't explain yourself to them. Just **starve them with silence** and **attention to better things**.

3. Remember, Replace

Speak what is true. Declare scriptures that root you in peace. Turn your attention to gratitude. **Fill your mind with good things. Light always replaces darkness.**

4. Pray Without Stressing

Prayer is not your last resort. It is your **first move**. It is not begging. It is **alignment**.

Stay in that rhythm. Let prayer shape your thoughts before fear can sneak in.

Prayer Is Not Panic

Too many people treat prayer like they're **begging for oxygen**, gasping for breath, moments from going under.

That is **not** the posture of power. That is **not** the voice of peace.

When you pray without stressing, you are telling your body, your brain, and your world: "I am already covered. God is already moving. I don't have to beg. I just have to stay connected."

That is the **language of spiritual authority**.

This kind of prayer doesn't just calm the heart. It brings **clarity**. It resets your **nervous system**. It centers your **energy** in the truth that everything you need is already in motion.

Prayer, when practiced this way, is **alignment, not anxiety**.

Permanent motivation is not born in a crisis. It is not fueled by pressure or panic. It is born in **peace**, sustained by **stillness**, and grown strong through **prayer that trusts instead of trembles**.

Don't Beg, Become

Someone once said: "Don't beg, become."

That's the shift. That's the transformation. That's what it means to **pray without ceasing**.

Not repeating desperate requests into the air, but **walking like the answer already lives in your bones**.

Begging says: "I hope He hears me."

Becoming says: "He already did."

What Science Calls Allostasis, Faith Calls Preparation

In neuroscience, there's a term for this process: **allostasis**.

It means your brain **predicts and prepares** for your body's needs before they arise.

That's right, your brain budgets energy and emotion **in advance** based on what it expects to happen.

If you expect **danger**, your body prepares for stress. If you expect **rejection**, your body prepares for isolation. If you expect **failure**, your body prepares for shutdown.

This is how many people arrive at chronic fear, doubt, and stagnation.

Their brain is constantly preparing for negative outcomes, creating the very physical and emotional states that make those outcomes more likely.

But here's the breakthrough:

If expectation can prepare your body for **negativity**, it can also prepare your body for **success**, **peace**, and **breakthrough**.

You must **consciously reverse** the process to return to your natural, fearless, spirit-filled state.

You Were Built to Believe

This is why **faith** is so powerful.

You weren't designed to live in a cycle of constant begging and uncertainty. You were designed to **receive divine guidance**, align your **expectations** with God's promises, and then **act like the answer is already unfolding**.

Prayer matters. But so does your **posture after prayer**. So does your **preparation**. So does your **willingness to become** the person who naturally receives what you've been asking for.

When you pray with **genuine faith**, you're not just making requests. You're programming your brain's predictive system to prepare for **blessing instead of disaster**.

You're training your body to expect **favor instead of failure**.

Stop praying over everything like you're unsure whether God hears you. Start believing like your prayers are **already being answered**, and let your brain prepare your entire system for **receiving**, not **lacking**.

Faith is the greatest form of spiritual intelligence. It doesn't just know how to ask for what you need. It knows **when to stop asking**, and start moving like the answer is already on its way.

***

"The principal rule of logic is to remain the principal.
Never let the principles of others override your authority.
When fear becomes the principal, true principles fall.
Be principal in your logic, and fear will never rule your principles. "

— **E. A.**

Chapter Five
LOGIC

- *"And be renewed in the spirit of your mind."* — **Ephesians 4:23, KJV**
- Understanding logic and the brain's capacity for renewal
- Research: how thought patterns physically reshape the brain
- Practical exercises: visualization, gratitude, prayer, forgiveness

Your mind isn't a concrete slab, it's a garden. Every thought plants a seed that either produces life or poisons the soil. Science now proves what Scripture declared centuries ago: your brain can be "renewed" and remade. You're not doomed to stay stuck. Every time you choose truth over fear, hope over despair, you are literally rewiring your future.

Logic: The Starting Point of Renewal

Let's begin by talking about logic, the foundation of every wise decision. Logic is not just cold calculation. It's a system of principles that uses reason to determine whether a conclusion is true or false. Using logic, a person gathers the available information, weighs it, and draws a conclusion based on the data at hand.

But here's the critical truth: even the sharpest logic cannot save you if the data is wrong. No matter how carefully you reason, no matter how disciplined your process, if the information you rely on is false, the conclusion will also be false.

Good reasoning + bad information = bad decisions.

When Facing Risks and Decisions

This matters most when you face significant risks in your life, when you stand at the start of something new and uncertain, whether it's launching a business, entering a relationship, pursuing a calling, or beginning a new chapter entirely.

These moments demand your clearest thinking because the stakes are high and the consequences will follow you for years. Your mind will naturally try to calculate the risks and rewards, weighing possibilities and probabilities to help you make the best choice.

This analytical process is healthy and logical, exactly what your brain was designed to do when facing important decisions. However, logic can only work effectively with the data it's given. And this is where most people encounter their first major obstacle.

In today's world, data is everywhere, flooding in from countless sources at unprecedented speed and volume. But while information is abundant, wisdom remains rare. The ability to distinguish between valuable insights and worthless noise has become one of the most critical skills you can develop.

This is why you must be extremely careful about where you get your information and whom you trust for guidance. The counsel you receive will directly influence the quality of your decisions, regardless of how intelligent or well-intentioned you might be.

Friends can be well-meaning but wrong, offering advice based on their own fears, limitations, or lack of experience in your particular situation.

Family members can be protective but limiting, wanting to keep you safe more than they want to see you grow, and potentially face the risks that growth requires.

Even experts can be knowledgeable but biased, influenced by their own experiences, financial interests, or the limitations of their particular industry or field.

Your future will rise or fall based not just on how well you think, but on what you allow yourself to think about, and who shapes your understanding of what's possible. The information you consume becomes the raw material for every decision you make, which means the quality of your sources directly determines the quality of your choices.

Your Information Source Shapes Your Future

Your information source is the most important factor when trying to reach a conclusion or make a life-changing decision. This matters more than your intelligence, your ambition, or even your natural instincts, because all of these qualities depend on having accurate information to work with.

Brilliant people make terrible decisions when they base them on flawed information, no matter how carefully they reason through the process. Ambitious people fail spectacularly when they pursue goals built on false assumptions about market conditions, personal relationships, or their own capabilities.

Even strong instincts can be corrupted and misled by constant exposure to negativity, limitation, or fear-based thinking from unreliable sources. When you consistently hear that something is impossible, risky, or foolish, your intuition begins to align with those messages rather than with your authentic inner guidance.

This is why choosing your information sources becomes as critical as any other major life decision you'll make. The voices you listen to literally reshape how you perceive reality, and what you believe is possible for your future.

Ask These Questions

Before accepting guidance from anyone, you need to evaluate their credibility and motives with the same rigor you'd use for any important business decision.

- What is their track record in this specific area, not just their general intelligence or success in unrelated fields?
- Someone might be brilliant in their profession but completely inexperienced in the type of risk or opportunity you're considering.
- What do they have to gain or lose from your decision, and how might their personal interests influence the advice they're giving you?
- Are they speaking from direct experience with similar situations, or are they making assumptions based on what they've heard or read?
- Have they ever taken the risks they're telling you to avoid, or are they counseling you from a position of safety they've never left?

The most dangerous advisors are often those who've never risked anything significant themselves, because they've protected themselves from failure, but also from breakthrough.

Choose your information sources as carefully as you'd choose a surgeon for a critical operation, because your future depends on the quality of the guidance you accept and act upon.

The Fear Filter in Business and Life

This problem becomes especially dangerous when it comes to business decisions and major life opportunities. Most people, when faced with a significant investment or career risk, automatically filter every decision through the fear-based thinking they've been absorbing for years from well-meaning but limited sources.

They don't consciously choose to think negatively, but their mental database is filled with cautionary tales, worst-case scenarios, and protective advice that prioritizes safety over growth. Before they can even properly evaluate an opportunity, their fear filter has already begun highlighting every possible way it could go wrong.

These mental warnings come rushing back in the form of familiar voices from the past. They'll remember parents who said, "It's too risky to start your own business."

They'll hear friends who warned, "It's too expensive to invest in yourself."

They'll recall family members who insisted, "People like us don't succeed at things like that."

Even teachers, coaches, or mentors, who meant well but were operating from their own limitations and fears, become part of this internal chorus of caution that drowns out possibility.

The result is a devastating internal conflict that sabotages decision-making before it even begins. Even when their logic clearly says, "This opportunity makes sense," their fear-conditioned emotions immediately respond with, "But what if it doesn't work out?" Their rational mind might recognize the potential for growth, profit, or positive change, but their emotional programming keeps them focused on protection rather than progress.

This fear filter doesn't just influence their decision, it often becomes the decision, causing them to pass up opportunities that could transform their entire future.

The first step to overcoming this pattern is recognizing when you're using a fear filter instead of making a balanced assessment. Ask yourself whether you're evaluating an opportunity based on its actual merits and your genuine capabilities, or whether you're simply rehearsing familiar fears that have nothing to do with your current situation.

Notice if the voices in your head belong to people who never took the risks you're considering, never achieved what you're pursuing, or never had to face the challenges you're facing now. Most fear-based advice comes from people who chose safety over growth and now want to justify that choice by convincing others to make the same decision.

Instead of letting fear make the decision for you, use it as information, while making space for possibility. Acknowledge the risks honestly, but also acknowledge the cost of doing nothing and staying where you are. Consider what you've learned, how you've grown, and what resources you have now that you didn't have when those fearful voices first programmed your thinking.

The goal isn't to eliminate fear but to prevent it from filtering out opportunities that align with your goals, values, and authentic potential for growth.

For Entrepreneurs and Everyone

I often use business examples throughout this book because it was originally going to be titled *Permanent Motivation for Entrepreneurs*. That was my initial plan, and I spent months developing content specifically focused on the unique challenges that entrepreneurs face when building something from nothing.

The entrepreneurial journey requires a special kind of mental resilience because you're constantly making decisions without guaranteed outcomes, fighting through rejection, and pushing past the limitations that others accept as normal. Business seemed like the perfect laboratory for understanding how permanent motivation actually works in high-pressure, high-stakes situations.

But as I continued to write, as the deeper truths about motivation and mindset became clearer, I felt compelled to expand the scope beyond just business owners. I realized that the same mental patterns that destroy entrepreneurs also destroy anyone trying to break free from mediocrity in any area of life.

The fear-based thinking that stops someone from starting a business is the same fear-based thinking that stops someone from pursuing a healthier relationship, changing careers, or stepping into their authentic purpose. I was led to leave the title open for all because these principles apply universally to anyone who refuses to settle for less than they're capable of becoming.

Because this is not just about business success or financial achievement. It's about life transformation. It's about renewing the mind and breaking free from limiting beliefs. It's about overcoming fear-based thinking in every area: work, relationships, personal growth, purpose, and faith.

The same mental strategies that help an entrepreneur push through the fear of failure can help anyone push through the fear of change, rejection, or stepping into the unknown.

Entrepreneurs face this battle against limiting beliefs and fear-based programming on a daily basis because their success depends on their ability to think differently than most people. But so does anyone trying to grow beyond the mental limitations of their past programming, family expectations, or cultural conditioning.

Whether you're building a business, rebuilding a relationship, pursuing a dream, or simply trying to become the person you know you're meant to be, you're fighting the same war against the voices that tell you to play it safe and stay small.

The principles in this book work for entrepreneurs because they work for human beings who refuse to accept limitation as their final answer.

When Fear Wears the Mask of Logic

Let's take a practical example that illustrates how fear disguises itself as reasonable thinking. Imagine someone starting a luxury clothing brand with genuine passion and a clear vision for their product. They're excited about the possibilities, have real talent for design, and have been working tirelessly to develop their brand identity and initial product line. Everything feels aligned and purposeful, and they're ready to take their business to the next level of professionalism and quality.

Then, in a moment of prayer or sudden inspiration, they feel strongly guided toward purchasing a DTF (Direct-to-Film) printer for their operation. Not just any basic printer, but a high-quality, $10,000 commercial-grade machine that would allow them to produce premium transfers in-house instead of outsourcing the work. The guidance feels clear and urgent, like a door opening at exactly the right time.

However, here's the challenging context that makes this decision so difficult: these new business owners haven't sold a single item yet. They've made exactly $0 in revenue from the business so far, and all they've done up to this point is spend money investing in designs, materials, branding, and business setup costs.

And now the inner guidance says clearly: *"Buy that printer."* The conviction feels strong and unmistakable, but it also feels financially impossible given their current situation. This creates the perfect storm for fear to disguise itself as reasonable business advice, making it nearly impossible to distinguish between wise caution and faith-killing doubt.

Before faith has a chance to formulate a response, fear immediately jumps in with what sounds like perfectly reasonable business logic:

"That's not a smart financial decision right now," it whispers urgently.

"You should wait until you have some revenue coming in to justify that kind of investment."

"How are you realistically going to pay for a $10,000 machine when you haven't made your first sale?"

"Be logical about this, buy equipment like that after you start making money, not before."

These objections sound completely rational and responsible, exactly the kind of advice any reasonable business mentor might give to an overeager entrepreneur.

Fear will even support its arguments by quoting popular business advice and success stories that seem to contradict the guidance:

"Didn't you read about that entrepreneur who started their clothing brand for under $100 and built it into a million-dollar business?"

"Every business expert says to start lean and bootstrap your way to success."

"Be reasonable, be cautious, don't move too fast or you'll end up like all those failed startups that spent too much too early."

It sounds like wisdom backed by research and experience. It sounds like the voice of logic protecting you from making a costly mistake.

But it's fear dressed up in the language of reason.

This is one of fear's most sophisticated tactics, presenting itself as practical wisdom when it's actually limitation disguised as logic. True wisdom considers both practical realities and divine timing, while fear-based thinking only focuses on worst-case scenarios and reasons why something won't work.

The challenge is learning to distinguish between genuine prudence that comes from wisdom and paralyzing caution that comes from fear, especially when both can sound remarkably similar on the surface.

Testing the Source

The key question isn't whether the guidance makes immediate financial sense, but whether it aligns with the authentic vision and long-term direction of the business.

Fear-based thinking always focuses on current limitations and potential problems, while faith-based thinking considers possibilities, timing, and the resources that might become available when you step forward in alignment with your authentic path.

Sometimes the most logical decision from a fear-based perspective is actually the most limiting decision from a growth perspective. And sometimes what appears to be an unreasonable risk is actually the exact step needed to unlock the next level of opportunity and success.

When Logic Conflicts with Calling

Here's the critical truth that separates those who break

through limitations from those who remain trapped by them:

Sometimes, what God calls you to do will directly contradict the available data.

This creates one of the most challenging situations any person of faith can face, because you're caught between what appears to be reasonable based on current evidence and what feels divinely inspired despite the lack of logical support.

Your brain, designed to keep you safe through careful analysis, will desperately search for information that makes the decision "make sense" according to conventional wisdom. And when it can't find enough proof to justify the step you're feeling called to take, fear immediately fills in the gaps with worst-case scenarios and logical-sounding reasons why you should wait for more certainty.

Fear's advice sounds perfectly reasonable: *"If you can't see the whole staircase, don't take the first step."*

This appears to be wisdom, why would anyone move forward without being able to see the complete path and calculate all the risks?

But God's approach to guidance operates on entirely different principles: *"Take the first step in faith, and I'll build the staircase as you climb."*

This requires a fundamentally different relationship with uncertainty, one that sees the unknown as a space for divine possibility rather than a collection of potential dangers.

The conflict between these two approaches creates the exact moment where your character and spiritual maturity are tested most severely.

Faith Is the Highest Logic

This tension between conventional reasoning and spiritual calling is precisely where mind renewal begins to take place.

Your old thought patterns, shaped by fear and limitation, automatically default to: *"Don't invest until the profit is guaranteed."*

This seems logical because it minimizes risk and appears to protect you from financial loss or disappointment.

But renewed thinking operates from a completely different framework: *"Invest when God says invest, trusting that the profit will follow obedience to divine timing and direction."*

This isn't reckless or financially irresponsible when it's genuinely rooted in spiritual discernment, rather than wishful thinking or impulsive emotion.

Faith is not the opposite of logic, **faith is the highest form of logic available to human beings.**

While conventional logic can only work with data that's currently visible and measurable, faith-based logic factors in elements that data analysis can never capture: the power of divine direction, the timing of opportunities that align with purpose, and the resources that become available when you're moving in authentic alignment with your calling.

This doesn't mean abandoning practical considerations or ignoring legitimate concerns. But it does mean recognizing that the most important factors in life-changing decisions often can't be quantified or predicted through conventional analysis.

Faith-logic integrates both practical wisdom and spiritual discernment, creating a decision-making framework that accounts for possibilities which fear-based thinking automatically dismisses as unrealistic or impossible.

The Fear-Friend: Neither Enemy nor Ally

This, my friends, is exactly how limitation disguises itself as wisdom in your life. Almost every major decision begins with genuine logic and careful consideration of your options and circumstances. But if you're not consciously aware of what's happening in your mind during this process, that logical analysis will gradually be hijacked by fear-based thinking masquerading as reasonable caution.

All the negative "help" from earlier examples, the cautious advice, the warnings about worst-case scenarios, the budget-minded thinking that focuses only on current limitations, will begin to sound like the voice of wisdom and experience. This transition from logical assessment to fear-based paralysis happens so subtly that most people never recognize when they've stopped making decisions based on possibility and started making them based on protection.

Sometimes this limiting voice comes from real friends and family members who genuinely care about your well-being but are projecting their own fears and limitations onto your situation. Most of the time, however, the most persistent and convincing version of this voice comes from one constant internal companion: your subconscious fear-friend.

This is not an external person trying to hold you back, but an internal program that has been shaped by years of disappointments, failures, and cultural conditioning about what's "realistic" for someone in your circumstances. It knows exactly how to sound helpful and concerned while systematically undermining your confidence and vision.

The Fear-Friend's Voice

This terrible "friend" has developed a remarkably familiar and persuasive voice that you've been listening to for years, without recognizing its true nature. It reminds you of your past failures in vivid detail, especially the ones that still carry emotional pain or embarrassment. It recalls other people's failures in similar situations, using their stories as evidence that your dreams are unrealistic or dangerous. It warns that every risk you take could potentially become a regret you'll have to live with for the rest of your life.

Most importantly, it always speaks in the tone of genuine concern and care, making it nearly impossible to recognize as the voice of limitation rather than love.

The fear-friend's favorite phrases sound like the advice of a caring mentor:

"I'm just trying to protect you from getting hurt again."

"Let's not repeat the mistakes of the past."

"Be smart about this, think about what you have to lose."

"Be safe, be cautious, be realistic about your circumstances."

It sounds helpful because it appears to be looking out for your best interests. It sounds reasonable because it's based on real experiences and genuine risks. It sounds logical because it can point to statistical evidence and cautionary tales that support its arguments.

112

But despite sounding like wisdom, it's actually the voice of limitation, programming you to choose safety over growth, protection over possibility, and fear over faith.

The True Nature of Fear

Here's the critical truth about this internal dynamic: your fear-friend is not really an enemy trying to destroy your life, and it's certainly not a true friend trying to help you succeed.

It's simply a problem that needs to be recognized and managed consciously, rather than allowed to operate automatically in the background of your decision-making process.

This voice is essentially a mental program built from old data, past experiences, and survival mechanisms that served you well when you needed protection from genuine dangers. But like outdated software running on a modern computer, it now creates more problems than it solves, because it can't distinguish between legitimate threats and growth opportunities that feel unfamiliar or challenging.

Your fear-friend is fundamentally a roadblock pretending to be a guardrail, offering protection that actually prevents you from reaching the destinations that would transform your life.

If you don't learn to take conscious control of this inner voice and evaluate its advice critically, rather than accepting it automatically, it will continue controlling your most important decisions.

Not because it wants to hurt you or keep you from succeeding, but because it's programmed to prioritize:

- Immediate safety over long-term growth
- Current comfort over future possibility
- Familiar limitation over unfamiliar breakthrough

Unchecked and unexamined, this voice will always lead you back to fear-based choices, no matter how logical and reasonable you try to be in your decision-making process.

Fear-Comfort: The Illusion of Safety

Your fear-friend will inevitably lead you into a psychological trap that I call *fear-comfort*, one of the most seductive and dangerous states of mind you can inhabit.

Fear-comfort feels safe because it eliminates the anxiety of making difficult decisions and facing uncertain outcomes. It feels reasonable because it's based on practical considerations and realistic assessments of your current circumstances. It feels protective because it shields you from the possibility of failure, rejection, or financial loss.

But this sense of security is completely illusory, creating a false sense of safety that actually keeps you trapped in limitation while convincing you that you're being wise and responsible.

Fear-comfort operates exactly like those fuzzy house shoes that look incredibly cozy and inviting when you first put them on. They appear soft and comfortable, promising relief from the discomfort of walking barefoot or wearing more structured footwear. They feel good in certain places, providing immediate comfort to parts of your feet that were previously exposed or pressured. They seem to offer the perfect solution to the problem of cold floors and tender feet, and initially, they deliver on that promise of comfort and protection.

But if you wear them long enough, you discover their hidden cost: they gradually rub painful blisters on your heels and toes, creating a slow, persistent discomfort that builds over time.

This is the perfect metaphor for how fear-comfort operates in your life.

Step by step, day by day, it keeps you in a state of slow, cringing psychological pain, not severe enough to make you run from the situation, but just persistent enough to keep you from walking freely toward your authentic goals and dreams.

You're not suffering dramatically enough to recognize the problem immediately, but you're also not living fully enough to experience the joy and fulfillment that comes from pursuing your real purpose.

Fear-comfort traps you in a middle ground of chronic dissatisfaction, disguised as reasonable contentment.

When Divine Guidance Conflicts with Fear-Comfort

This is why it becomes so challenging when God places something bold on your heart, like investing in that $10,000 printer or pursuing any other opportunity that requires you to step outside your current comfort zone and financial safety net. Your entire system of fear-comfort will activate to protect you from what it perceives as dangerous or unrealistic, flooding your mind with logical-sounding reasons why you should wait, be more cautious, or choose a safer alternative.

The guidance may feel clear and urgent, but your fear-friend will immediately begin generating counterarguments that sound like wisdom and responsibility.

In these moments, you must silence the mental noise and create space for spiritual discernment rather than emotional reaction. Be still with the guidance you've received and honestly ask: **"Is that You, Lord, or is this coming from my own desires or fears?"**

This requires developing the spiritual maturity to distinguish between authentic divine direction and wishful thinking, impulsive emotion, or unconscious rebellion against your current circumstances. When you've genuinely sought clarity, and the answer is unmistakably yes, then you must be prepared to act with the kind of boldness that transcends conventional logic and embraces faith-based decision-making.

Acting with Bold Faith

When you receive clear divine guidance to move forward, the instruction is simple but challenging: *buy, move, act*, not with fear, hesitation, or reluctant obedience, but with the boldness of someone who already possesses the successful outcome.

This means making the investment or taking the risk with the same confidence you would have if you could already see the future results of your obedience. It means operating from faith rather than fear, from abundance rather than scarcity, and from trust rather than anxiety about how everything will work out practically.

116

"Buy like you are rich" doesn't mean being financially irresponsible or ignoring practical considerations. It means making decisions from a mindset of abundance and divine provision, rather than limitation and human reasoning.

And here's the profound spiritual principle: *you will become rich*, not necessarily because of the specific item or investment itself, but because you demonstrated the faith to obey divine guidance when it conflicted with conventional wisdom. Obedience to authentic spiritual direction always produces blessing, though it may not always look exactly like what you expected or arrive on the timeline you anticipated.

The Wealth of Obedience

When you intelligently act rich, even if you don't yet have the physical money in your bank account, you are demonstrating that you're already rich in the most important currency available to human beings: *obedience and faith.*

This doesn't mean being financially reckless or making impulsive purchases based on wishful thinking. It means making strategic investments and decisions from a mindset of abundance and divine guidance, rather than scarcity and fear-based limitation.

Acting rich intelligently means recognizing that your current bank balance doesn't define your true capacity for creating value, generating income, or attracting the resources needed to fulfill your authentic purpose. It means making decisions based on your *potential and calling*, rather than your current circumstances and limitations.

Faith-led action creates a powerful alignment between your choices and divine provision, one that operates on principles most people never understand or experience.

When you step forward in obedience to clear spiritual guidance, even when it doesn't make complete sense from a purely logical standpoint, you position yourself to receive resources, opportunities, and solutions that wouldn't be available through conventional planning and risk management alone.

This process gradually renews your mind by replacing the old *fear-comfort*; that false sense of security that comes from playing it safe and staying small, with a *new comfort* based on trust in divine timing, provision, and guidance. This new comfort is infinitely more secure than the illusion of safety that comes from hoarding resources or avoiding all risks.

You begin to understand that you are not rich because of what's currently sitting in your account, but because of who is ultimately guiding and directing your account, and your entire financial future.

This shift in perspective transforms not just how you make financial decisions, but how you relate to money, opportunity, and provision in general.

When you know that the same divine intelligence that orchestrates the universe is also orchestrating your financial life, you can make bold moves and strategic investments with confidence and peace rather than anxiety and desperation.

Your security comes not from the size of your savings, but from the strength of your relationship with the Source of all abundance.

This doesn't mean that practical financial wisdom

becomes irrelevant, or that you should ignore budgets, planning, and responsible money management. Rather, it means your financial decisions are guided by both *practical wisdom* and *spiritual discernment*, allowing you to recognize and act on opportunities that fear-based thinking would automatically reject as too risky or unrealistic.

You learn to distinguish between *genuine divine guidance* toward strategic investments and *impulsive desires* driven by materialism or emotional needs.

The result is a financial life that's both spiritually aligned and practically successful, because you're making decisions from *wisdom* rather than fear, *abundance* rather than scarcity, and *faith* rather than anxiety about uncertain outcomes.

The Dream-Stealing Prison of the Logical Mind

Do not allow fear, logic, reason, reality, the idea of "being smart," or doubt to hold you back.

As strange, and even humorous, as it may seem, the people who cling to these voices as their guides rarely reach greatness or freedom.

They succeed in safety.
They succeed in smallness.
But they do not succeed in purpose.
They do not succeed in destiny.
And they do not succeed in the life they were uniquely created for.

These voices promise protection,
But they often deliver paralysis.
They present themselves as wisdom,

But they quietly suffocate vision.

The logical mind, when untrained, does not build dreams.

It *cages* them.

True freedom and growth begin when you stop letting these internal guards dictate your every move.

You are not here to stay safe. You are here to become something powerful. Something amazing.

_____

_____

_____

_____

_____

_____

_____

_____

_____

The Anatomy of the Mental Prison and the Physical Prison

Let's take a deeper look at the structure of captivity, both mental and physical.

The average prison cell no longer uses bars to restrain its occupants. Modern cells are four solid walls and a metal door. This design doesn't just restrict movement; it restricts the senses. Gone is the open visibility that bars once offered. A barred cell allowed inmates to see, breathe, and even feel like they had space, however small. Now, the only view is through a small window, often no larger than 28 by 33 inches. It's confining. It's smothering.

That is exactly how the mental prison works. It doesn't rely on chains, it relies on structure. It limits your perspective. It compresses your hope.

Below is a breakdown of this invisible prison, brick by brick:

1. **Fear is the prison itself:** It traps your imagination and shrinks every possibility. It convinces you to stay small and trapped.
2. **Logic is the warden:** It walks the halls of your mind, enforcing restrictions and labeling your dreams as risky or unrealistic.
3. **Reason is the jail cell:** It's the story you tell yourself about why it's better to stay where you are, even if it hurts.
4. **Reality is the steel door:** It's heavy, final, and loud. It tells you that no one escapes, that what you see is all there is.
5. **Being smart is the tiny window:** It allows a glimpse of the outside. It whispers that more is possible but warns you not to try.
6. **Doubt is the food tray slot:** It feeds you just enough to survive. It keeps you alive, but never lets you thrive.

You are not in a cell made of concrete and steel. You are in a cell made of beliefs. But the key has always been in your pocket. The moment you choose to believe differently, the door begins to open.

Why This Metaphor Matters

Everyone can relate to this image. Going to jail and

losing freedom are among humanity's greatest fears. It triggers the deepest survival instincts.

But here's the truth: many people are already imprisoned, not by steel bars, not by guards, but by a mindset built from fear, logic, reason, reality, being smart, and doubt.

Their mental prison feels like wisdom. It sounds like common sense. It looks like caution. But it's actually a slow, comfortable death of dreams. It convinces you to stay small, to stay safe, to stay in your place.

You are not in physical chains, but your thinking is shackled. The cell is invisible, but the limits are real. You walk through your days with freedom in theory, but bondage in practice.

If you don't confront this inner prison, your goals become visitors you never invite in. Your dreams become posters on the wall instead of seeds blooming outside the door. And worst of all, your potential dies in silence.

No alarms.

No keys turning.

Just resignation.

But there is another way.

Freedom Requires New Logic

If you want to escape this prison, you must begin by renewing your mind, not in theory, but in action. Freedom is not something handed to you. It is something claimed by those who dare to think differently.

You must reprogram your thoughts and tear down the

patterns that have convinced you smallness is safety.

You cannot wait for permission to grow. You must challenge the mental warden, the inner voice that says, *"Play it safe,"* even when safe is killing your purpose.

That door holding you in? It is only as strong as the beliefs that built it. It will not break until you decide it no longer belongs in your life.

Reject the false "wisdom" that tells you to be cautious with your dreams. You are not being responsible by playing small. You are being irresponsible with your potential.

True wisdom is knowing when to leap.

Real logic is learning to listen beyond fear.

Freedom is not reckless. It is obedience to your purpose.

Playing small is not humble. It is dangerous.

It is a slow betrayal of everything you were born to become.

So Why Keep Yourself in That Mental Jail?

Why stay locked up when the door has already been opened?

More importantly, why let others guard that door for you with their opinions and doubts?

Every time you let someone else's fear masquerade as wisdom, you tighten the chains around your own future.

Fear wears a lot of disguises. It dresses up as logic. It pretends to be caution. It even calls itself love and concern. But at its root, it is still fear.

And if you agree with it, you accept the terms of the prison without ever questioning the sentence.

It is not the fear itself that keeps you trapped. It is the agreement.

The moment you listen, the moment you nod and say, *"Maybe they're right,"* you close the door on your own destiny.

You stop before you even begin.

But here's the truth you have to remember:

The door is already open. God unlocked it long ago.

What's holding you now isn't the lock, it's the habit of hesitation. And habits can be broken the moment you choose to walk out.

What Healthy Risk Really Looks Like

Taking a healthy, faith-led risk is not always about making a huge investment. It does not have to look like spending ten thousand dollars on a printer.

Sometimes, it is simpler. It might mean signing up for a course that stretches your thinking. It might mean buying the tools that prepare you for the vision you have been given.

It could be having a bold conversation that shifts everything. It might even be launching the idea that has been on your heart, long before you feel fully prepared.

Readiness is rarely a feeling.

More often, it is a decision you make in faith.

Healthy risk looks different for everyone, but the principle is the same: it is movement in the direction of your calling, not based on comfort, but based on clarity.

It is listening to God and acting, even if your knees shake as you do.

So whatever God is telling you to do, **that** is your next step.

Do not delay it.

Do not water it down.

Do not wait for applause.

Trust the voice that gave you the vision, and take the step that aligns with it.

Cast Logic Aside When Faith Speaks

When divine instruction arrives, logic must step aside.

Not because logic is useless, but because logic only operates within the limits of what is known. It builds its case from what has already happened, what others have tried, and what makes sense on paper.

Faith, however, speaks from what is possible beyond evidence. It draws from what is unseen but destined.

When God speaks, the instructions often won't align with logic, because logic cannot comprehend miracles.

If Abraham had listened to logic, he never would have left his home. If Moses had listened to logic, he never would have stood at the Red Sea with nothing but a staff.

Divine instruction defies reason so that the outcome can reveal the source.

You were not called to live by human wisdom alone. You were called to live by divine direction.

When faith speaks clearly, logic becomes the background noise. Let it fade, and move forward in obedience.

Faith Operates in the Realm of What's Possible

Faith operates in the realm of what is possible. It does not ask for proof. It does not wait for all the pieces to line up. It moves in alignment with divine instruction, even when logic begs you to wait.

"Cast logic away." Not permanently, but in moments when it tries to chain you to your past instead of guiding you into your purpose. Logic has its place, but it is not the master of your calling.

When purpose calls, you don't need explanation.

You don't need everyone's permission.

You don't need the approval of those who never had the courage to move.

You only need obedience.

Obedience is the doorway to freedom. It is the choice to trust what is higher, wiser, and eternal. When logic hesitates, obedience walks forward. And when you walk in obedience, everything else eventually catches up.

Faith operates in the realm of what is possible. It does not rely on what is already proven. It moves with purpose, not with hesitation.

Cast logic away, not forever, but long enough to stop it from chaining you to your past. Logic is useful, but not your guide when faith is speaking.

Obedience is the true doorway to freedom.

Not explanation.

Not permission.

Not consensus.

Obedience.

When you obey what you know is right in your spirit, you move forward. And that movement breaks the limits fear tries to place on your life.

Brave People Use Logic the Right Way

Brave people use logic the right way. They treat it like a fire extinguisher hanging on the wall in the kitchen. It's there for emergencies, but it doesn't stop them from turning on every burner.

They cook with the biggest pots. They let the flames rise high because they know what they're doing.

The extinguisher is nearby, just a few steps away. It's ready if things get out of control, but it doesn't dictate every move. It doesn't stop the meal from being made. It doesn't stand in the way of the fire that brings transformation.

This is how logic should be used in a life of purpose: not as a barrier to boldness, but as a tool of safety when wisdom calls for it. Logic can protect, but it should never paralyze.

True courage isn't found in avoiding all risk.

It's found in moving forward with clarity, faith, and the quiet understanding that you are equipped to handle the fire when it rises.

Healthy Risk Requires Bold Action and Backup Plans

Bold action comes first. Logic stands ready, but not dominant. It doesn't take the lead. It doesn't steer the ship. It waits in the background until it's truly needed.

Throw logic out the window, but keep it on a rope. When a real emergency arises, pull it back in. Let it serve you. Do not become a servant to it.

Wear logic like a chain tucked neatly under your shirt. It's not for show. It's not for approval. It's there for protection, close to your chest, invisible to the world.

Only reveal it when a healthy risk truly requires caution. That's how visionaries move. That's how entrepreneurs grow. That's how faithful, purpose-driven people renew their minds, by knowing when to trust faith, and when to let logic catch the fall.

14 Motivational Thoughts

- Bravery uses logic as a tool, not a master.
- Safety devices don't cook the meal. They protect the cook.
- Logic belongs in the background until needed.
- Faith leads. Logic assists.
- Risk is reckless without wisdom. But wisdom is brave.
- Boldness grows when fear shrinks.
- The fire extinguisher hangs ready. It doesn't control the heat.
- Your purpose deserves flames, not constant caution.
- Throw logic out. Keep it close. Use it wisely.

- Permanent motivation balances courage and care.
- The mind renews by acting, then adjusting.
- Fear leads to freezing. Faith leads to forward.
- Logic cannot create. It can only protect what's created.
- Purpose requires movement. Logic follows movement, not the other way around.

Fear Is a Drug

Fear is a drug. Not like nicotine or cocaine, because those don't lie to you.

Fear pretends to be your friend. It dresses up as wisdom. It talks softly, calmly, and says, *"I'm just looking out for you."* But behind the smile, fear is always angling to keep you small. It doesn't just show up, it settles in, acting like it belongs.

Fear is worse than any addiction because it's free and everywhere. You don't have to seek it out. It finds you. While nicotine waits for your craving, fear arrives uninvited and sells you a story about staying safe. While cocaine empties your wallet, fear quietly empties your future, then convinces you that nothing was taken.

Even when you think you've beaten fear, it hides in the corners. It waits for a weak moment, and when it sees you hesitate, it steps in again. Fear does not respect victory, it only respects replacement. You can't outthink it or outrun it. You must override it. And you do that with belief, discipline, obedience, stillness, and spiritual alignment.

The truth is, fear thrives in silence and hesitation. That heavy, almost warm feeling in your chest right before a big decision or life change? That is fear's way of showing you who's still in control. It tells your body, *"Stay right here. Don't move. Something might go wrong."* And while nothing may go wrong in that moment, everything stops when you obey it.

Fear pretends to protect you, but it is the most consistent thief of purpose. It has kept more people poor than poverty itself. It has broken more relationships than betrayal. It has killed more ideas than rejection ever could. Not because people were incapable, but because fear whispered, *"Play it safe,"* and they did.

Think of the clown from a horror movie. Friendly on the surface. Waiting underneath to drag you under.

That is fear.

It smiles. It softens. Then it strikes. At first it charms you, then it calms you, then it claws at you. And by the time you realize what it is, it has already wrapped around your motivation like a net.

You've felt it before, that strange warmth in your chest. That heaviness right before a leap. The second before you start something new. It's like a fake heart attack made out of hesitation. No alarms go off. No one around you notices.

It's just you. Still.

Stuck.

Paralyzed by something you can't even explain.

And while that feeling may not stop your heart, it will stop your future. It doesn't crash into you like a car. It doesn't scream. It just whispers, *"Not yet."* Then it whispers again the next day. And again the next week. Until time has passed, and all you have is a memory of what you were about to do.

Fear looks like protection. But if we're being honest, it's not. It's a prison.

It doesn't just hold you back from danger.

It holds you back from growth.

It will keep you broke in more ways than money.

It will rob your peace.

It will drain your purpose.

It will ruin love before it starts.

All while telling you it is keeping you safe.

Fear, when you really examine it, is nothing but an assumption.

Not a fact.

Not evidence.

Just something you accepted as truth without asking one question.

It is a guess you treated like a guarantee.

And because you didn't challenge it, it became your limit.

You predict what might go wrong, and fear takes that prediction and runs with it. Suddenly, you are not responding to reality. You are reacting to a guess. A scenario that hasn't happened becomes the force that controls your next move.

This is how fear works. It doesn't wait for evidence.

It just needs a whisper of uncertainty.

And here's the twist:

You didn't choose fear.

You made a prediction, and fear offered to help.

It stepped in like an uninvited guest and promised to protect you.

You didn't invite it, but you also didn't stop it.

So it moved in.

That's how fear takes control, by offering to lead when no one else is in charge.

Fear only has power when you let assumptions go unchallenged. And most people never challenge them. They call them common sense. They wrap fear in words like "caution" or "practicality."

But at its core, it's still fear.

Unchecked.

Unchallenged.

And now in the driver's seat.

When fear takes over your protection, it smothers you. It's like someone grabbing your head and shoving it underwater just to keep a drink from hitting your face.

One is a splash.

The other is suffocation.

And fear always chooses the most extreme form of control, while calling it safety.

Fear is that toxic friend who holds you underwater while saying, *"Don't worry. I'm teaching you to swim."*

You would have recovered just fine from the drink.

But now you are gasping for air.

You are drowning in a safety that was never safe.

You are watching your progress sink, while fear smiles and calls it love.

So ask yourself: *Are you being protected?*

Or *are you being quietly destroyed?*

If you don't confront fear daily, it's not just holding you back, it's actively hurting you. Fear is not a quiet passenger. It is a driver. And if you allow it to linger, it will steer your entire life. It doesn't need your permission, just your silence.

Ridding your life of fear is not a side task.

It is not something you squeeze in between meetings, chores, or scrolling through your phone.

It is the first work.

The real work.

The foundational work that makes everything else possible.

Because if fear stays in the room, it runs the room.

You might get a breath.

You might even get a breakthrough.

But you will never be free.

Fear knows how to let go just long enough to make you

think you've won.

Then it tightens the leash.

Fear will loosen its grip just long enough to fool you into trusting it. But you're still in the river. Still caught in the current. Still one unexpected wave away from going under again.

And that is not freedom.

That is survival.

And survival is not the goal.

Until you learn to rule fear, it will keep ruling your decisions. It will influence how you spend your money, who you trust, how much you love, and how far you go.

It does not stop unless you stop it.

And that begins the moment you say: **"No more."**

This is not about being fearless. It is about no longer living under fear's permission. It is about no longer asking it for clearance every time you want to move forward.

The next version of you cannot be built with fear at the table.

The Slow Drowning

Fear won't always choke you with dramatic, obvious attacks that force you to fight back immediately. Sometimes, it gives you just enough air to keep drowning slowly, creating a false sense that you're managing fine when, in reality, you're suffocating gradually. It straps on a fake life jacket of routine, safety, and reasonable choices, then tells you, **"This is what security looks like."**

And you get used to this state of barely surviving instead of truly living. The numbness becomes normal. The constant low-level tension fades into background noise. The daily sense of something vital missing becomes just part of adult life.

You stop dreaming about possibilities because dreaming requires energy you no longer have. You stop caring deeply about outcomes because caring leads to disappointment. You don't hate people, but you don't love them with the intensity you once did either. You're not quite hopeless, but you've become hollow in the places where passion used to live.

This is what happens when you let fear stay too long in the driver's seat of your life. You no longer feel the sharp pain of crisis, because you've adapted to chronic limitation. But you also don't feel anything that makes life worth living with enthusiasm and purpose.

The fake life jacket keeps you from drowning completely, but it also prevents you from swimming toward the shore, where real life is waiting.

Breaking the Surface

The first step to breaking free from this slow drowning is recognizing that what feels like safety is actually a form of drowning.

Ask yourself: *When was the last time you felt genuinely excited about your future, rather than just relieved that you're getting by? When did you last take a risk that made your heart race with possibility rather than fear?*

If these questions reveal that you've been surviving rather than thriving, you're ready to remove the fake life jacket of false security and learn to swim again, toward something that actually matters to you.

Friends and Family or Friends and Foes

Let's talk about the most underestimated threat to your motivation: the people closest to you.

Not enemies.

Not critics.

Family and friends.

When they reject your dreams, it doesn't just sting, it digs. These are the people you thought would cheer first. But instead, they plant doubt, even if they say it with a smile.

It's not always intentional. But your brain doesn't care about intention. It registers betrayal.

The psychological weight of disappointment from loved ones is heavier than any rejection from strangers. When someone close to you downplays your vision, it echoes louder than a million trolls online.

That kind of rejection rewires your ambition.

It makes you second-guess what God already confirmed.

Suddenly, you're not just fighting fear, you're fighting the grief of being unseen.

And that grief can kill momentum if you let it.

You expected encouragement. Instead, you got silence, skepticism, or worse, sarcasm. And it cuts deep because it feels personal.

But here's the truth: Most people close to you can only see who you've been, not who you're becoming. That's not your problem to fix. It's not your burden to carry.

Don't shrink your dream to make it easier for them to digest.

Your calling is not their responsibility.

You must learn to separate support from permission. Not everyone who loves you is meant to walk with you. Some are meant to watch. And some will only understand when the vision is fulfilled, not before.

That's okay. Keep going anyway.

Their doubts don't disqualify you.

Their limits don't define you.

If you wait for them to believe in your dream, it may never start. But if you believe anyway, you might wake them up.

We start to believe that friends and family are our biggest enemies, not because they truly are, but because their rejection hits harder than anyone else's.

They know us. We've shared meals, holidays, and childhoods. So when they doubt our dreams, it doesn't feel like disagreement, it feels like betrayal.

But in reality, they're no more of an enemy than a stranger who just can't see your vision. **The pain is in the placement, not the person.**

What hurts isn't just their words, it's your expectation of them. You thought they'd see your growth. You thought they'd recognize your calling. But most people don't have the capacity to support what they don't understand.

That doesn't make them evil. That makes them limited. And you can't base the trajectory of your dream on someone else's lack of vision.

The real trap is thinking you must share your dreams with them. But your deepest, most sacred desires aren't for public discussion, they're for spiritual confirmation.

Too often, we offer what's holy to people who are unprepared to honor it. That mistake doesn't make them an enemy. It just means you shared something sacred in a space that wasn't ready.

And that's a mistake you can fix.

So don't confuse confusion with betrayal.

And don't take silence as sabotage.

Most friends and family do what they've always done, react from their reality, not yours.

That doesn't mean they get to make your decisions. It just means you may have to walk some steps without applause.

Trust that when the dream becomes visible, some people who doubted will double back in support. But even if they don't, you're still called.

Sharing your dreams is not casual. It's intimate. It's spiritual.

You're handing someone the blueprint to your soul when you open up about your vision. So naturally, you expect them to meet you with enthusiasm, encouragement, even awe.

But it hits differently when friends and family don't reciprocate that energy. Suddenly, they feel less like support systems and more like obstacles.

The disappointment isn't just emotional, it's chemical. Studies in motivation and psychology show that social affirmation boosts dopamine, which fuels momentum.

So when your dreams are met with a shrug, or worse, a smirk, your internal system slows down.

It's not weakness.

It's human.

And the more emotionally connected you are to the person rejecting your dream, the heavier that emotional impact becomes.

For someone trying to build permanent motivation, this is one of the most dangerous blows you can take, not because it can't be recovered from, but because it often leads to withdrawal.

You stop sharing.

You stop building.

You retreat into silence, not because the dream isn't real, but because the rejection felt too personal to risk again.

That's how great visions die in rooms full of familiar faces.

But here's the truth you must hold:

Their reaction does not reflect the worth of your dream.

It only reflects their capacity to recognize it.

Your calling doesn't need their applause.

Your motivation doesn't need their mirror.

Grieve the rejection if you must, but get back up and guard your dream with stronger boundaries.

Because not everyone who loves you is equipped to hold what you carry.

This disconnect happens for one simple reason: **you expected them to feel what you feel.** You thought they'd match your energy, your fire, your vision. But it's not their dream, it's yours. And they weren't given the same glimpse of what's possible. So when they don't reflect your passion, it feels like rejection.

But it's not rejection. It's just misalignment.

Dreams are deeply personal. They're **whispers from God to you**, not conference calls. When you try to make others feel what only you were meant to carry, you're setting yourself up for disappointment. It's not their fault, but it's also not their responsibility.

Your dream wasn't planted in a crowd. It was planted in you. And it's your job to protect the soil.

Don't demand excitement from people who weren't there when God gave it to you. Most people won't understand until they see the fruit, and that's okay. Let them taste the fruit later, but don't hand them the seed too early.

Not because you're hiding, but because you're honoring what's sacred.

Some things aren't meant to be shared. They're meant to be shown.

So move forward without needing validation. Let go of the hope that they will hype you up. You don't need hype, you need discipline. Their enthusiasm might come one day, but your results will speak louder than their early silence ever did.

Keep building. Keep becoming.

You were never meant to convince them, only to obey what you were shown.

Crowds don't fulfill dreams. Dreams are realized through **faith in God**, not through the applause or support of others. Friends and family may cheer or stay silent. They may stand beside you or disappear. But your dream is not theirs to carry. It is not their burden, their blueprint, or their responsibility.

God placed it in you. And He alone knows how to bring it to life.

It's a blessing when you have supportive people around you, that's grace. But don't build your foundation on it. If you're waiting for everyone to believe before you move, you'll never move. **God has a habit of working with the willing, not the approved.** You weren't called to a group project; you were chosen for a purpose.

When friends and family fall short of your expectations, don't take it personally. **They're not blocking your dream;**

they were never holding it.

And that's good news.

You don't own your dream, **God does.** He's the one writing the story, orchestrating the timing, and assigning the right people for each chapter. **Trust Him more than you trust their reactions.**

So walk in faith, not frustration. Release the pressure to explain yourself. Stop trying to get everyone on board.

The people who are meant to walk with you will show up. And the ones who don't? **They were never necessary.** Let God build the team. You just stay obedient.

That's how dreams become reality.

***

Remember this: You don't need to go out collecting résumés for who gets to help you with your dream. That's not your job. It's not your company, it's God's vision.

And HE does the hiring.

He appoints, anoints, and sends people right on time, so no interviews are needed.

So stop asking for help from people God hasn't assigned. **When He gives the vision, He also controls the staffing.**

Too many people waste time trying to *"build a team"* before they've built faith. You don't need a hype crew, you need obedience. You don't need applause, you need alignment.

The truth is, some of the people you're trying to recruit would only slow you down. Not because they're bad people, but because they weren't called to this work.

God doesn't need résumés. He doesn't scan qualifications. He directs hearts. He turns strangers into allies and doubters into witnesses. He sends the right help when it's time, and never a second too early.

You don't have to force it. You don't have to beg.

The ones who are meant to help you will hear it in their spirit, not just from your mouth.

So stop performing. Stop pitching your dream like it needs approval.

The only endorsement that matters has already been stamped on your spirit.

Trust that. Protect it.

Let God be the recruiter, the manager, the supplier.

And you? You stay faithful to the assignment.

***

Renew your mind. That's where it starts and where it stays.

You have to keep reminding yourself:

God is the Boss. He's the one who planted the dream, gave the assignment, and opened the door. You didn't hustle your way here, you were led.

And when the breakthrough happens, when the vision becomes reality, **don't forget the hand that built it.**

When people start calling you a leader, don't let that go to your head. Let it become your responsibility. There's a difference.

You're not here to flex authority. You're here to

serve with clarity.

That's how real leaders are born.

Not by trying to be the "boss," but by staying connected to who the real Boss is.

Too many people lose themselves in the success of their dreams. They forget who carried them when it looked impossible. They trade calling for control.

But if **God gave you the dream**, only He can sustain it.

Leadership under His direction doesn't look like dominance. **It looks like stewardship.**

So stay humble. Stay grounded.

Let success make you more obedient, not more entitled.

Let influence sharpen your listening, not your ego.

You're not the source. You're the vessel.

And if you live like that, you'll never run dry.

You won't just be a boss.

You'll be the kind of leader the world has been praying for.

🔑 Final Declaration: "I Know Who the Boss Is"

- I am not the source of my strength.
- I am not the author of my calling.
- I am not the boss, I am the steward.
- I walk by vision, not validation.
- I build with faith, not fear.
- I lead by listening, and I live by truth.
- My dreams do not own me, **my God does**.

- And because I remember who the Boss is,
  I will never lose what He gave me to carry.

🧠 Reflection Prompt: Before You Lead, Who Are You Following?

1. Have you been trying to take control of a vision God gave you to steward?
   o Where have you tried to *"play boss"* instead of staying aligned with the real Boss?
2. What does leadership look like when it's led by humility instead of ego?
   o Write down 2–3 traits of the kind of leader you feel called to become.
3. How will you remind yourself daily that your dream belongs to God, not the world, not your ego, and not your critics?

Chapter Six
Finding Your Purpose

- *"But the God of all grace... after that ye have suffered a while, make you perfect, stablish, strengthen, settle you."* — **1 Peter 5:10, KJV**
- Psychological research on post-traumatic growth
- Pain as a catalyst, not a conclusion
- Actionable ways to mine meaning from suffering

Pain isn't proof that you're losing, it's often a sign that you're leveling up. God promises that suffering isn't the end; it's the setup for strength, stability, and power. Psychologists call it *post-traumatic growth.* The Bible simply calls it *redemption.* Your wounds don't have to end your story. They can become the very pages that save someone else's life.

The Question We're Trained Not to Ask

Let's take a deep look into pain. Not a surface glance. Not a passing thought. A real, honest examination.

Most people never do this because facing pain feels harder than carrying it. Ignoring it seems easier. Burying it seems smarter. But when you bury pain, you're not hiding it, you're planting it. And **planted pain always grows.**

Which Comes First: Pain or Unhappiness?

Here's the question: **Does being unhappy produce pain? Or does pain cause unhappiness?**

We could argue that point forever. Philosophers have. Psychologists have. Preachers have.

But maybe there's no real difference at all.

Maybe unhappiness and pain are not cause and effect.

Maybe they're simply different names for the same experience.

Pain is unhappiness the body can feel.

Unhappiness is pain the mind can think.

Both are signals. Both are messengers. And both are **invitations to change, not punishments.**

Society does not reward reflection. It rewards distraction. It tells you to numb the pain. Shop it away. Drink it away. Work it away. Entertain it away.

The goal is not healing. The goal is silence.

Because if you stop to feel it, you might start to ask hard questions. You might start to challenge the race. You might stop performing the roles that keep the machine running. And the system depends on your exhaustion and compliance.

But here's the deeper truth: **pain is not your enemy. It's your guide.**

It shows up when something needs to be seen.

It doesn't come to destroy. It comes to instruct.

It's not punishment. It's an invitation.

Pain does not come to break you. It arrives to direct you. It does not come to keep you small. It comes to push you forward.

What you feel is not the end. It's the signal that something greater is trying to begin.

Your Business Is a Mirror of You

This book is not just about wealth. It is about building better entrepreneurs by first building better people.

You cannot separate your success in business from your growth as a person. They are connected, and always will be.

Your business will never outgrow you. If you are stuck mentally, emotionally, or spiritually, your business will eventually reflect that. Every limitation you carry becomes a ceiling your business cannot break through.

Your success in the marketplace will always reflect your success in personal growth. Your mindset, your habits, and your level of self-awareness are the real profit margins.

Fix those, and everything else begins to flow.

That's why this chapter, and this entire book, focuses first on mindset, purpose, and emotional resilience.

Before you make a dollar, you must become someone who can carry the weight of the responsibility that comes with it.

Business Is Not Just About Money

Business is not just about money. It's about impact. It's about the legacy you leave in the lives of the people you serve.

If profit is your only goal, you are building on a weak foundation. A business should be an extension of your community. It should reflect your values, your purpose, and your desire to create something meaningful.

It should **contribute**, *not just consume.*

It should **solve problems**, *serve people, and reflect your* **highest values**.

These are not extras or luxuries, they are the heart of any lasting business.

Your **integrity is your real brand.**

Business isn't just a tool to extend your bank account. If that's all it is, the business may succeed financially for a time, but your employees and community will suffer. And when people suffer, systems break.

Eventually, that failure will leak back into the financial side as well. Culture erodes. Teams fall apart. Customers lose trust. *The cracks show.*

Purpose sustains, while profits fluctuate. Build your business on purpose, and even in uncertain times, it will have something solid to stand on.

Leave the Past Behind

If you bring your unresolved past into entrepreneurship, you are building on shaky ground.

You cannot create something solid when the foundation within you is still unsettled. Your business will only rise as high as your internal stability.

Unhealed trauma becomes business drama. It shows up in your decision-making, your team dynamics, and your ability to trust. It clouds your vision and makes small problems feel like personal attacks.

Unaddressed fear becomes leadership paralysis. You hesitate when you should act. You overthink when you should delegate. You play it safe, not because it's wise, but because fear disguises itself as strategy.

Old insecurities become toxic business relationships. You attract chaos. You tolerate disrespect. You confuse validation with partnership. And before long, you're surrounded by people who reflect your wounds, not your worth.

You are almost guaranteed to fail if you carry these burdens into your journey. Not because you lack intelligence or ambition, but because you're trying to lead a new life with old wounds.

That conflict will eventually catch up with you.

Heal first. Then build. Address the emotional leaks before you install the plumbing.

That's not just smart business. That's **permanent motivation.**

Your Purpose Is Bigger Than Your Paycheck

When your business becomes an expression of your healed self, not your hidden pain, everything changes.

The work feels different. The pressure lifts. You're no longer creating from a place of scarcity or survival. **Your energy changes.**

People can feel the difference. Clients respond not just to what you offer, but to the peace and confidence behind it. You're not selling out of desperation, you're serving and helping.

Your clients change. You begin to attract people who match your growth, not your grief. They respect your boundaries, value your time, and recognize your worth without needing to be convinced.

Your results change because you're no longer sabotaging success with self-doubt. You trust your instincts. You move with clarity. You stay consistent, because you're no longer running from yourself.

Permanent motivation is not about working harder. It's about working from a place of healing, clarity, and purpose.

That's what keeps you moving when the excitement fades. That's what makes your success sustainable.

14 Motivational Thoughts

- Your business cannot grow beyond the limits of your healing.
- Profit cannot cover the cracks in a broken foundation.
- A business built on purpose will survive what money cannot.
- The community you serve is the soil. Purpose is the seed.
- Unhealed pain turns into unwise decisions. Choose healing first.
- Leadership without clarity creates followers without direction.
- Your past teaches you. It should never control you.

- Customers feel your energy before they see your product.
- Permanent motivation requires permanent growth.
- Money follows meaning, not the other way around.
- Your worth is not in the revenue. It's in the results you create for others.
- Money-driven businesses burn out. Purpose-driven businesses endure.
- The person who grows is the person who succeeds.
- Your business should be a mirror of your healed, purposeful self.

Unhappiness: The Great Creativity Blocker

Nothing good consistently comes to those who are unhappy. That's not a punishment, it's a principle. Unhappiness alters your energy, your thinking, and your decisions. It pulls you into a cycle that repels clarity and attracts confusion.

This isn't a curse, it's cause and effect. Just like planting a seed in poor soil, you cannot expect growth when your internal environment is toxic. The soil of your mind determines what ideas take root.

The stress that comes from being unhappy clouds your judgment. It narrows your vision and fills your thoughts with doubt. Even the most basic tasks feel heavy when you're carrying emotional weight.

Unhappiness makes even simple solutions seem impossible. You can have the right answer right in front of you and still talk yourself out of acting on it, not because you can't do it, but because your emotional filter says, *"Not today."*

It turns opportunities into threats. Instead of seeing doors, you see danger. Instead of trying, you overthink. The very things meant to grow you begin to look like risks not worth taking.

It shuts down the part of the brain responsible for innovation and risk-taking. A fearful mind cannot create; it can only survive. And survival mode will never build the life you were meant to live.

Fear Magnets and Destructive Risks

Unhappy people become magnets for fear. They attract it, absorb it, and unknowingly surround themselves with others who confirm their fear. Fear becomes their atmosphere, not because they enjoy it, but because it's what they know. **Familiar pain often feels safer than unfamiliar peace.**

This mindset leads them to avoid healthy risks, even the ones that could bring growth, healing, or financial opportunity. Instead, they take destructive risks. They pursue toxic relationships, make impulsive decisions, or chase shortcuts that offer temporary relief but lead to long-term setbacks.

Destruction feels more predictable than the unknowns of success.

They begin to tell themselves that peace is unrealistic, that happiness is for other people, and that success is somehow beyond their reach. These thoughts aren't rooted in truth, but in repeated disappointment.

The more they rehearse these beliefs, the more real they

feel. And soon, the pursuit of progress is replaced by the maintenance of survival.

Permanent motivation cannot thrive in an environment ruled by fear. It requires an intentional shift in mindset, a daily refusal to agree with limiting beliefs. **Unhappiness must be challenged, not coddled.** Until that happens, even the best business strategy or life plan will collapse under the weight of unresolved fear.

The Corner Cutters

Worse still, unhappy people often struggle to remove negative, fear-driven influences from their lives. They stay close to those who reinforce small thinking and self-doubt. These voices don't challenge them to grow. They simply echo the same fears they already believe.

They keep the corner cutters nearby.

You know the type… The ones who always seem to offer advice that *sounds* smart but leads nowhere. They dress up bad judgment as caution, convincing others to stop before they even start.

These are the people who justify quitting by calling it maturity. They speak against risk because they fear the discomfort of progress. They call fear wisdom and wear their limitations like armor.

To them, safety is the highest goal, even if it means standing still forever.

Their words sound like protection, but they are prisons. They offer comfort not because they care, but because they fear being left behind. And so, they hold you in place with soft warnings and hard limits.

To grow, you must recognize their influence and walk away.

The Cycle Ends When You Choose It

This cycle does not break itself.

It does not fade quietly or dissolve with time.

It continues until you make a conscious, deliberate decision to stop feeding it.

Fear and unhappiness will lead as long as you allow them to.

At some point, you must decide.

You must say, *"I will no longer allow unhappiness and fear to lead my life or my business."*

That choice is not easy, but it is always available. It is not a one-time declaration. It is a daily commitment.

Permanent motivation begins at the moment of that decision. It begins when you stop entertaining fear-driven voices and start reclaiming the part of you that is courageous, creative, and whole. The voice that wants to build, serve, grow, and thrive.

You do not have to be perfect to make this choice. You just have to be willing.

The moment you commit to that willingness, you are already on your way to lasting change. The shift is quiet, but powerful, and it always begins within.

14 More Motivational Thoughts

- Unhappiness clouds vision. Clarity begins with a choice to release it.
- Fear and creativity cannot share the same space.
- Destructive risks feel safer because they are familiar. Choose the unknown.
- Corner cutters love the safety of fear. Growth makes them uncomfortable.
- Advice rooted in fear sounds wise but leads to regret.
- You were not created to survive small. You were designed to build big.
- Fear is a magnet. Purpose is a shield.
- Unhappiness does not protect you. It imprisons you.
- The brain opens new doors when peace replaces panic.
- Permanent motivation requires permanent pruning of negative voices.
- Healthy risk is not danger, it's destiny calling.
- Cutting corners cuts confidence. Take the full path.
- Your best ideas live beyond the borders of fear.
- Freedom begins when you choose better influences.

Fear Disguised as Wisdom

I knew a blogger once.

She had a vision. A business idea. A dream that whispered to her daily: *"You can do this. You can work for yourself. You can build wealth and freedom through the internet."*

She wanted to invest in a $2,000 camera setup to start

her blogging business.

It wasn't just about the camera.

It was about starting something real.

Something serious.

Something hers.

Her excitement was clear. Her motivation was pure. She saw opportunity. She saw possibility.

And then, as so many do, she made a mistake.

She told her friends.

The Dream Killers Arrive

One by one, they shot her dreams out of the sky.

She expected support, maybe some advice. Encouragement, even. But instead, she got negativity and fear dressed as guidance.

"That's too much money for a camera."

"Why not just use your iPhone?"

On the surface, it sounded practical. But it wasn't. It was fear speaking through people who were too afraid to admit they had stopped dreaming long ago.

I stood by and watched the spark leave her eyes.

Frustration crept in.

Then hurt.

Then doubt.

Her once-excited, motivated face tightened with

hesitation. She tried to explain herself.

"The camera is better than the iPhone. Spending two thousand dollars to make a million is a good investment."

But the fear kept talking.

"You haven't made a million yet."

"Do you know how hard it is to make a million dollars?"

Of course, they didn't know. They had never tried. They had never built anything that asked more of them than comfort and safety.

They only knew how to cut corners. How to shrink their vision. How to hide behind fear and call it wisdom.

The Pain of Shrinking Dreams

The biggest pain in life is not failure. It is shrinking your dream to fit someone else's fear.

That day, my friend stood at that painful crossroads. She had to choose between trusting her vision or absorbing their anxiety.

So many people face this without even realizing it. They trade boldness for approval. They downsize their purpose to fit the comfort zones of people who never left theirs.

The truth is simple: **dreams do not survive in cages built by fear**. And they will never soar if you keep asking permission to fly.

The lesson is clear, **never ask small thinkers for permission to dream big**. They can't see what you see. And they're not supposed to.

14 Motivational Thoughts

- Fear-advice sounds practical, but it produces paralysis, not progress.
- People who haven't built will always question builders.
- Small thinkers measure cost. Visionaries measure potential.
- Your dream will be heavy at first. Don't ask light-lifters to carry it.
- Negativity is not wisdom; it's the defense of comfort zones.
- Fear disguised as caution will suffocate your future.
- Support doesn't always come from where you expect. That's normal.
- Protect your dreams from the cheap opinions of the untested.
- $2,000 to make a million is called an investment. Fear calls it a waste.
- Every entrepreneur faces the crossroads: conform or create.
- Small thinkers don't mean harm, but their limits can become yours.
- Permanent motivation requires selective listening.
- Don't explain your dream to those who fear the journey.
- Your vision doesn't need a vote. It needs action.

God Sees No Difference Between a Dollar and a Billion

As soon as I saw her doubt creeping in, I pulled her aside.

I told her what too many people never hear: **"Stop listening to those people. Stop sharing your dreams with small thinkers. Their fear is not your future."**

The words hit her, not like hype, but like clarity.

I reminded her that to God, a million dollars is no different than a single dollar. **The size of the blessing is never the issue. The size of your belief is.** The limit is never in the outcome. It's always in the expectation.

Most people can believe for a dollar. They can believe for a paycheck. They might even stretch their hope enough to believe for a small raise. But the moment you speak about believing for millions, they step back, not out of hate, but out of limitation.

They withdraw their support not because they want you to fail, but because they can't see what you see. They can't feel what you feel. And that's okay.

It was never their vision to carry. It was yours. And it still is.

Here's the deeper truth: **if you believe God can make a way for you to receive a dollar, then you must also believe He can make a way for you to receive ten million, or even a hundred million.**

The number doesn't change the power of God. It only changes your belief about what is possible.

To God, numbers mean nothing. He doesn't deal in limits. But to us, numbers mean everything. We assign weight and difficulty to them. That's the problem. We make the blessing heavy when it was meant to flow.

Your mindset, your belief system, creates a vibration. It sends out an energy that the world responds to.

If you carry paycheck vibrations, you attract paycheck outcomes. But when you align with the energy of abundance, you begin to draw in opportunities that match that belief.

This isn't mystical thinking. It's spiritual alignment with practical effect. It's the natural law of faith, focus, and readiness.

As Matthew 9:29 says, **"According to your faith be it unto you."**

Permanent motivation requires **permanent belief in what's possible**, even before it arrives.

14 Motivational Thoughts

- God does not measure in dollars. He measures in faith.
- What you expect, you attract. What you fear, you delay.
- Small minds fear big visions. Protect your dream.
- A paycheck mindset produces paycheck results.
- Million-dollar thinking starts before million-dollar earnings.
- Don't share divine dreams with people living in doubt.
- God's provision is not limited by human math.
- Energy flows where faith grows.
- Your vibration tells the world what you're ready for.
- Paycheck thinking clings to comfort. Wealth thinking embraces risk.

- Every blessing starts with belief. Doubt delays destiny.
- Stop lowering your vision to match others' fears.
- Permanent motivation means permanent faith.
- Your dream is between you and God, not you and the crowd.

Pain Can Be Power: The Science of Post-Traumatic Growth (PTG)

There's a scientific term that describes what faith has taught for generations. It's called *Post-Traumatic Growth*, or *PTG*. PTG is the study of the power some people tap into after surviving traumatic or deeply challenging life experiences. It goes beyond recovery. It's more than bouncing back, it's the beginning of transformation.

This transformation isn't just about healing wounds. It's about becoming someone new. PTG shifts your desires. It rewrites your vision. It changes your perspective, your understanding, your beliefs, and your values. It creates a new foundation built not on what broke you, but on what awakened within you.

Through PTG, people gain increased resilience. They discover greater personal power. They develop deeper empathy. And they walk with a clearer understanding of themselves, the people around them, and the world they live in. It is not just a rebound, it's a rebirth.

It almost sounds like fiction. Like a comic book transformation from a regular person to a super-being. But it's not. It's real. It's human. And yes, it's divine.

PTG is what happens when a person who once lacked vision begins to see clearly, not just the world, but the emptiness of its temporary rewards. What once seemed important now feels hollow. And what once felt out of reach now feels like destiny.

It's when someone who struggled to feel for others now desires to live by the golden rule, not because it's expected, but because their heart has changed. They no longer just sympathize, they empathize. They see people through the lens of shared humanity, not judgment.

It's when a formerly closed heart opens wide. When the one who was once self-focused now feels called to help, to serve, to bring healing where there was once harm. Pain, when faced and understood, doesn't shrink your life. It expands your reach. It increases your power.

Pain does not come to define your defeat. It comes to define your next chapter. That's what PTG represents. It is not guaranteed. Not everyone chooses to grow from their pain. But the invitation is always on the table.

The Bible puts it this way:
"But we glory in tribulations also: knowing that tribulation worketh patience; and patience, experience; and experience, hope."
(Romans 5:3–4, KJV)

Science calls it *Post-Traumatic Growth*. Scripture calls it *spiritual maturity.*

I call it **purpose in the middle of pain**.

14 Motivational Thoughts

- Pain is not a prison. It's a portal to new power.
- Your trauma was not wasted. It was a seed for growth.
- What crushed you once can now create clarity.
- PTG proves pain can produce purpose, not just scars.
- Empathy is born when pain is understood, not avoided.
- You are not the person you were before the struggle.
- Every loss can lead to wisdom if you allow it.
- Worldly desires shrink when spiritual vision grows.
- Pain didn't end you. It introduced you to your next chapter.
- Strength is not found in avoiding pain but transforming it.
- PTG is not recovery. It's resurrection.
- What you survive can become what you serve others with.
- Permanent motivation grows when pain is turned into purpose.
- Your struggle wasn't meaningless. It was a calling in disguise.

Pain as the Superhero Origin Story

If this still sounds impossible, think about the stories we tell in movies and comics. **Pain has always been the**

beginning of the hero's journey. It's the moment everything changes. In almost every great origin story, the transformation starts with trauma. The suffering becomes the spark.

It sounds dramatic, but these stories come from real human experiences.

A spider bite transfers power to the body.

A shock of electricity awakens something dormant.

There is pain.

There is fear.

But then something shifts. The power arrives. The vision sharpens. The purpose becomes clear.

Yes, there is always a cost. Yes, there is fear at first. But then the pain begins to fade. And what remains is not just survival, but strength. Not just recovery, but clarity. Not just endurance, but power.

PTG (Post-Traumatic Growth) is the real-world version of the superhero story. Your trauma was the bite. Your crisis was the surge. Your hardship was the explosion.

But the pain wasn't the end. **It was the transfer of power. Your superpower.**

What Hurts Now Can Heal Later

The temporary trauma caused by the spider bite or the electrical surge fades in comparison to the benefits of having new abilities.

In the same way, the pain of your past may still echo,

but it no longer defines you. It introduced you to strength, wisdom, empathy, and clarity you never had before.

Pain was not the end of your story. It was the **beginning** of your transformation.

14 Motivational Thoughts

- Pain is not just a wound. It's the doorway to awakening.
- Every hero's story begins with struggle.
- Your trauma wasn't punishment. It was preparation.
- The bite stings. The shock hurts. But the power lasts.
- You carry strengths you didn't have before the struggle.
- What broke you once built resilience now.
- Your pain introduced you to your purpose.
- The world honors survival. You are called to transformation.
- PTG is not fiction. It's faith meeting growth.
- Your scars are not signs of defeat. They are proof of progress.
- Heroes don't avoid hardship. They rise because of it.
- Permanent motivation is born when pain produces power.
- The sting fades. The growth remains.
- You are not who you were. You are stronger than you imagined.

Don't Wait for Trauma to Transform You

Here's what I'm telling you:

You do not have to wait for trauma to change your life. Transformation can begin with a decision. A choice. Not a breakdown. Not a disaster. Not a final straw. Just a moment of clarity where you decide to live differently… to lead yourself forward instead of being dragged by pain.

Most people wait until the crisis comes. Until something snaps. Until they cannot bear another day of pressure. Then, and only then, do they move. That becomes their turning point. But it doesn't have to be yours.

That path is common, but it was never the only one. The design for your growth does not require destruction. It was always meant to begin with **faith**, not fear. With **vision**, not panic.

You were never meant to learn only through suffering.

Trauma comes when we ignore the invitation to grow. It pushes us in the direction we were already meant to go. But what if you stopped waiting for the push? What if you started walking now?

You can change by choice, not by collapse. And that choice is always available.

Choose Change Before Crisis Chooses You

I'm not saying you'll avoid every traumatic event, even if you choose to grow. Pain is part of life. We all face it in different ways. But here's the truth you need to hold on to: **you don't have to wait for pain to decide who you will become.**

You don't need trauma to push you into clarity. You

don't have to let struggle be the only thing that wakes up your strength. You don't have to let crisis be the only voice that calls you into purpose.

You can choose now. You can decide who you are before life tries to decide for you.

Most people wait until everything falls apart. They wait for the breakdown, the loss, the collapse. But **you are not most people.** You don't need to hit bottom to rise. You can rise from vision, from choice, from conviction.

This is how **permanent motivation** is born, not in chaos, not in catastrophe, but in the quiet moment when you choose to step forward, not because you must, but because you are ready.

14 Motivational Thoughts

- Growth is not a punishment. It's a choice.
- Pain can push you. But wisdom can pull you.
- Don't wait for a crisis to create clarity.
- Your superpowers are waiting. You don't need permission.
- Trauma introduces change. Conscious choice accelerates it.
- You were designed for growth by decision, not just reaction.
- Every day is a chance to evolve without suffering.
- Pain may teach. But purpose can lead.
- The strongest people move before life moves them.
- Permanent motivation starts with permanent awareness.
- You don't have to break to break through.

- Your future self is a decision away, not a disaster away.
- Waiting for trauma delays your destiny.
- The power to change is already in your hands.

Your Superpowers Are Forged Through Hardship

People develop these superpowers in different ways.

For some, it begins with a near-death experience. For others, it comes through a serious illness. It might arrive in a season of loss or through the relentless weight of hardship. No matter the path, **pain has a way of reshaping the soul**.

Tough times melt away the stubborn wax of selfishness. They strip down pride. They reveal what truly matters, and what never did. The illusions fall away, and what remains is something softer, stronger, and more real.

Suffering invites compassion. Struggle builds patience. And pressure uncovers purpose. Those who walk through the fire with open eyes come out carrying light.

This is how some of the kindest, most grounded people are formed, not by comfort, but by endurance. Not by praise, but by perseverance.

Find Your Superpowers Now

You don't have to wait for crisis to claim your power. You don't need a breakdown to spark your breakthrough. You can grow strong before the storm. You can build peace before the pressure.

Find your superpowers on the journey to becoming the

better person you already want to be. They are not hidden in tragedy. They are revealed in daily choices, in intentional growth, and in quiet courage.

Entrepreneurship is not just a business pursuit. **It's a personal transformation.** Every challenge you face is an invitation to grow, not just your income, but your integrity.

Use every obstacle to build strength. Use every setback to build resilience. Let generosity, discipline, and purpose shape the foundation you build on.

Entrepreneur or Money Seeker?

Ask yourself a question most people avoid: **"What am I? Am I an entrepreneur or just a money seeker?"**

There is a big difference.

Entrepreneurs are creators. They are givers. They wake up thinking about how to solve problems and improve the lives of others. They build with purpose. They invest in the future.

Money seekers are takers. They chase profit without meaning. They want quick wins, not lasting impact. Their work often serves only themselves while pretending to serve others.

One path builds a legacy. The other builds distrust.

You have to choose which one you want to be.

The Trap of Greed

Most business failures, and much of the pain that comes with them, can be traced back to one root: **greed.**

Greed is a deceptive companion. It always wants more, gives less, and never knows when to stop. Even when it wins temporarily, it always loses in the end.

Greed will convince you that success is about accumulation, not contribution. But make no mistake, **greed is a trap disguised as ambition.** It pushes people to chase without purpose and to consume without consideration. And that kind of drive never lasts.

Losers are not people who lack money. They are people who chase money with no mission behind it. They measure worth by wealth, but live empty lives. And in that pursuit, they lose themselves.

Without purpose, **profit becomes poison.** It corrodes your values and clouds your vision. It makes you forget why you started. And if you're not careful, it turns your dream into a transaction.

14 Motivational Thoughts

- Hardship melts pride and molds purpose.
- Your superpowers are not found in ease but in endurance.
- Tough seasons awaken strengths that comfort cannot.
- Entrepreneurs create. Money seekers consume.
- Service builds. Greed breaks.
- Your value is in what you give, not what you gather.
- Pain is not punishment. It's preparation.
- Resilience is a superpower forged in fire.
- Greed promises gain but delivers emptiness.
- The generous endure. The selfish collapse.

- Business is a mirror of your motives.
- Permanent motivation grows when greed dies.
- Character outlasts cash.
- Choose purpose. Choose power. Choose the better path.

Chapter Seven
Permanent Motivation: A New Way to Live

- *"Wherefore seeing we also are compassed about with so great a cloud of witnesses... let us run with patience the race that is set before us."* — **Hebrews 12:1, KJV**
- Moving beyond hype-based motivation.
- Living in a cycle of faith, prayer, purpose, and renewal.
- Vision casting: A lifetime of permanent motivation.

Hype burns out. True motivation doesn't. The race you're called to run isn't a sprint of emotion, it's a marathon of conviction. Permanent motivation comes from living anchored in something deeper than feelings.

You need purpose, prayer, and a renewed mind. You don't need another caffeine buzz of "get hyped" energy. You need a foundation that storms can't shake.

Please hear this clearly and don't ignore it: Forget the get-rich-quick schemes. Forget the internet gurus promising fast money through cheap tricks. That mindset is a trap.

The only way to change your life is to learn a real skill. And right now, there's no excuse not to.

We are living in the most accessible educational era in history. Major universities are offering free online courses, and they're not fluff, they're the same classes offered to paying students:

- **Harvard University**: *CS50: Introduction to Computer Science, The Health Effects of Climate Change* (edX)
- **Stanford University**: *Machine Learning, Algorithms: Design and Analysis* (Coursera)
- **MIT**: *Intro to Computer Science with Python* (OpenCourseWare)
- **UC Berkeley**: *The Science of Happiness, Bitcoin and Cryptocurrencies* (edX)
- **Yale University**: *The Science of Well-Being, Financial Markets* (Coursera)

If you have internet, you have access. It's that simple.

Now, if you're serious about not being left behind in the AI economy, and not stuck in fear or financial lack, then you need to focus on these five high-demand AI skills that people are already monetizing today:

1. **Machine Learning:** Teaches systems how to learn from data and improve automatically. It powers recommendation engines, fraud detection, and more. Big money, real value.

2. **Natural Language Processing (NLP):** Gives machines the ability to understand and generate human language. Think chatbots, language translators, AI copywriting, this is already reshaping communication.

3. **Computer Vision:** Enables machines to "see" and interpret images and videos. Used in healthcare imaging, autonomous vehicles, retail, and security systems.

4. **Prompt Engineering:** The skill of crafting precise inputs (prompts) to get high-quality outputs from large language models like ChatGPT.
5. **Data Analysis and Visualization:** The ability to interpret, clean, and display data in ways people understand is essential for every company making decisions based on metrics, which means every company.

✦ **Bonus Skill**: *AI Ethics and Governance:* Organizations desperately need thinkers who understand how to build and deploy AI responsibly.

***

Learning is not the same as mimicking. Watching YouTube and copying someone's hustle will never match what happens when you truly understand a skill.

You have to learn, apply, and own it.

This book is not about hype. It's about **lasting change**. Permanent motivation doesn't come from inspiration alone, it comes from action, discipline, and investing in your mind.

You don't have to beg for freedom. **You build it.**

Skill by skill. Day by day.

The opportunity is in front of you. **Take it.** Learn while it's free. Grow while it's possible. Your future is still under construction. **Start building.**

The Big Bang Theory (of Life and Fear)

I call it my Big Bang Theory. Actually, no, I call it my Big Bang *Fact*, because you can take it to the bank when it's applied correctly. Both banks: life's bank and the wealth bank.

This theory, this fact, holds the same flowing currency that the wealthiest banks recognize: **Energy. Anticipation. Control over fear.**

And it starts with a simple truth: **There's no real difference between fear and anxiety, only between preparation and surprise.**

Let's break it down.

Think about the Fourth of July. What's the first thing that comes to mind? For most people, it's barbecue, family, laughter... and fireworks. The Big Bang. It's a traditional ritual. People don't fear it, they anticipate it. In fact, they look forward to it.

We gather, eat too much, drink a little too much, and then wait in joyful suspense for someone, often the least qualified person in the group, to light the fireworks. And we laugh about it, because it's familiar. We know it's coming. We expect the bang. Even the loudest explosions rarely make anyone jump.

But let's change the scene.

Now imagine you're walking through a quiet park at night. No crowd. No laughter. No family barbecue.

Out of nowhere... **BANG!** A firework goes off just a few feet behind you. Same sound. Same decibel level. But this time, your heart jumps into your throat. Your pulse spikes. Your body reacts with fear.

Why?

Because you didn't expect it.

The bang itself didn't change. Your awareness did. Your preparation, or lack thereof, turned what would have been excitement into anxiety. The bang became a threat because it surprised you.

The Fear-Anxiety Connection

Here's the crucial point most people miss about their emotional responses to challenging situations:

Fear and anxiety are not separate emotions that require different coping strategies.

They are the **same physiological reaction**, shaped entirely by your expectations about what's going to happen.

The difference between feeling excited anticipation versus paralyzing dread has **nothing to do with the actual event itself**, and everything to do with how mentally prepared you are for what's coming.

When you expect the bang and have prepared for it, your brain interprets the approaching challenge as something manageable. Your adrenaline rises in a healthy way that sharpens your focus and enhances your performance. You stay alert but confident, ready to handle whatever comes next. You might even enjoy the rush of adrenaline because you know you're equipped to succeed.

When you don't expect the bang, or haven't prepared for it, your brain automatically interprets the same situation as **immediate danger**. This triggers panic, helplessness, and an overwhelming desire to run away or hide.

It's the **same external event**, producing the **same internal chemical response**, but your lack of preparation causes your brain to label it as a threat instead of an opportunity.

***

The only variable that determines whether you feel **confident excitement** or **paralyzing anxiety** is how mentally and practically **prepared** you are for what's ahead.

This principle applies to every area of life where you face uncertainty or challenge.

- Job interviews become exciting opportunities when you've prepared thoroughly, but anxiety-inducing ordeals when you haven't.
- Starting a business feels like an adventure when you've researched and planned, but like jumping off a cliff when you haven't done the groundwork.

The key to transforming anxiety into excitement is simply changing your relationship with preparation and expectation.

No Obstacle You Prepare For Should Scare You

This is the foundation of what I call the **Big Bang Fact**: *Nothing you can anticipate should genuinely scare you into paralysis or avoidance.*

When you can see a challenge coming from a distance, you gain the most powerful advantage possible in any difficult situation, **time to prepare**. This preparation time allows you to transform what could be a shocking, overwhelming experience into a manageable, even exciting opportunity for growth and progress.

Starting a business, starting over completely in life, or taking serious control of your health, relationships, and finances are all significant "bangs" that you can see coming long before they arrive. They might feel large and intimidating when you first consider them. They might seem loud and disruptive to your current comfortable routines. But they are not surprises that catch you completely off guard, they are predictable parts of any meaningful journey toward improvement and authentic living.

If you prepare for these challenges systematically, if you anticipate the specific obstacles and difficulties they will bring, the paralyzing fear begins to fade naturally. Instead of panic and avoidance, you develop focus on solutions and readiness for action. You might even discover excitement about the possibilities that lie on the other side of the challenge.

This transformation happens exactly like it does on the Fourth of July, when you know the fireworks are coming, you can position yourself to enjoy the show rather than being startled by unexpected explosions.

The Key: Shift from Reactive to Proactive

Shift your mindset from **reactive surprise** to **proactive preparation**.

- Research what others have experienced in similar situations.

- Identify the specific skills and resources you'll need.
- Create contingency plans for the most likely obstacles.

When you've done this groundwork, challenges become puzzles to solve rather than threats to survive.

Prepare. Position. Proceed.

If you know the fireworks are coming, you don't panic or run away in fear. Instead, you stand at a safe distance that protects you from harm. You might put your fingers in your ears to muffle the sound. You might close your eyes during the brightest moments or brace yourself for the impact.

But you do not abandon your position and miss the show entirely.

This is exactly how you should approach every significant goal in your life. Treat challenges and obstacles as **predictable fireworks**, not unexpected disasters. Anticipate the difficulties that will inevitably arise. Prepare for them by gathering the knowledge and resources you'll need. Learn through books, courses, and conversations with people who have navigated similar challenges.

Position yourself at a distance that is both **safe and bold**.
Get close enough to take meaningful action, but far enough from unnecessary risks to maintain stability.

Then proceed with confidence, knowing that you've done everything possible to prepare.

- **Preparation builds competence and confidence.**
- **Positioning ensures you're approaching your goal**

from the right angle with proper support systems.

Why Fear Feeds Procrastination

Most people procrastinate **not** because they're lazy, but because they turn their backs on the inevitable "bang." They refuse to face the challenges they know are coming. They act as if denial will make the difficulties disappear or become less intense.

This avoidance creates **false comfort** while making the eventual confrontation much more difficult.

Turning away from anticipated challenges only **amplifies** the fear when it finally arrives. You spend time imagining worst-case scenarios instead of developing practical strategies for handling them.

However, facing challenges directly, and preparing for them, **shrinks the fear** before it grows into paralyzing anxiety. When you know what's coming and you've prepared for it, the "bang" becomes manageable background noise rather than an overwhelming explosion.

The Funny Truth about Fearful People

We all know people who still flinch at fireworks, even when they can clearly see the fuse being lit and know exactly when the explosion is coming. But here's what's interesting:

Do they leave the party and go home to avoid the discomfort? *No, they don't.*

They stay at the celebration. They jump and flinch at each bang. But they **remain present** for the entire show.

That's the most important lesson about courage:

Courage is not the absence of fear, but the decision to stay engaged despite feeling afraid.

Naturally timid people can build genuine resilience through repetition and deliberate exposure to the things that make them uncomfortable. They flinch at the first few fireworks, then recover their composure more quickly. They wait for the next explosion with slightly less anxiety than before.

Each round of exposure reduces their fear response and increases their confidence in their ability to handle discomfort. If people who are naturally more fearful can develop this kind of resilience through simple practice, then **anyone** can learn to face their anticipated challenges with greater courage.

Stop Running from What's Coming

Your next breakthrough, business opportunity, important relationship decision, or bold life change is like a firework waiting to go off in your personal sky.

You can't avoid the bang when it's time for it to happen. You can only choose whether you'll be **prepared for it** or **caught off guard**.

The smart approach is to:

- Face what's coming directly
- Prepare for the intensity
- Smile, knowing that you're ready for whatever follows

Position yourself strategically **before** the explosion happens so you can **control your experience** instead of letting it control you. Prepare your mind, gather your resources, and develop your skills **before** the pressure arrives.

Your new life, the one you've been imagining and working toward, is waiting just beyond the next major challenge you face. And beyond that challenge, there will be **another** opportunity for growth and **another** chance to prove your resilience.

This is simply how life works And **fear will never win** when you've taken the time to prepare yourself mentally and practically for what's ahead.

Train Your Fear. Command Your Energy.

Fear and anxiety are **not your enemies**. They are **untrained energy**. Shape them. Use them. They respond to **preparation** the way fire responds to a spark.

The bang you expect will never have the same power as the bang you deny. Fear grows in the shadows. Shrink it with awareness. Procrastination is not laziness. It's fear in disguise.

Turn and face it. Even if you tremble, you are still stronger than what you fear.

Prepare. Position. Proceed.

This is the **cycle of the unafraid**. This is how you build permanent motivation in a world built on uncertainty.

The first bang is always the loudest. But once you survive it, the next becomes familiar. **Familiarity tames fear. Experience builds courage.**

The Strategy of the Strong

- Stillness before action.
- Clarity before movement.
- Wisdom before ambition.

This is how the strong stay ready for every bang that's coming.

Don't run from the noise of life.

Learn to dance in it.

Learn to expect it.

Learn to prepare for it.

Then the fear loses all control.

Your fear feeds on surprise. Starve it with preparation. Break the cycle of panic by anticipating every challenge that could come.

Life will not go silent. Challenges will not stop. But when you expect the noise, you own it.

You command it.

*You **outlast it**.*

Each bang is a doorway.

You can jump back in fear...

Or walk through in power.

The choice is always yours.

People fear what they refuse to prepare for. And people conquer what they choose to anticipate.

You were built to conquer. The bang is coming. It always will.

But fear it?

No.

Welcome it.

Master it.

And use it to fuel your next breakthrough.

Reflection Exercise: Facing Your Bangs

Use this exercise to turn fear into focus and prepare for the "bangs" you know are coming.

Step 1: Name Your Bangs

List three things in your life right now that feel overwhelming, intimidating, or uncertain, things you've been avoiding or worrying about.

Example:

- Starting my business
- Rebuilding a broken relationship
- Facing a financial challenge

Your List:

1. _____
2. _____
3. _____

Step 2: Identify the Fear

For each "bang," write down the specific fear you

associate with it.

Example:

- **Business:** Fear of failing and losing money.
- **Relationship:** Fear of rejection or further hurt.
- **Finances:** Fear of not being able to recover from debt.

Step 3: Prepare to Hear the Bang

For each fear, write one action you can take now to prepare.

You don't have to solve the problem today, just take one step toward readiness.

Example:

- **Business:** Schedule a call with a mentor.
- **Relationship:** Write down what I would say in a healing conversation.
- **Finances:** Review my budget and set a small goal.

Step 4: Write Your Declaration

Finish with this bold statement, write it in your journal or say it aloud: **"I expect the bangs in my life. I will not run from them. I will prepare for them, face them, and master them. Fear will not control my story. I will."**

Your Business Fireworks Have Already Been Lit

So, if you want to start a business, **stop waiting** for the "perfect moment." That fuse has already been lit. The bang is coming whether you're ready or not. The market is moving. The opportunities are shifting. Technology is advancing. Customers are searching.

The question is not, "Should I start?"

The question is, "Will I be ready when the fireworks explode?"

Prepare for the bang.

That means:

- ✓ Start now.
- ✓ Don't quit.
- ✓ Don't give up.
- ✓ Don't expect perfection, expect growth.

Others have already lit the fuse, competitors, trends, demand. The fuse is burning down whether you stand still or step forward. Trust God. Lean into the fire.

Keep yourself permanently motivated, not by chasing the rat race, which will only wear you out, but by grounding yourself in **belief**.

Belief is your fuel. Not speed. Not comparison. Belief.

Your passion, your skills, your story, **that's the flame.** And it's already burning inside of you.

The following steps are the fireworks waiting to ignite. They are not impossible. They are **invitations.**

Beginner's Best Practices: Start Your Small Business

Here's a clear, realistic, bang-proof plan for beginners.

Don't overcomplicate. Don't stall. Start.

🔥 Step 1: Clarify Your "Why"

Why this business? Why now?

Write it down. If your "why" isn't bigger than your fear, the bang will scare you back into silence.

🔥 Step 2: Choose One Simple Product or Service

Start small. One offer. One solution.

Test demand. Don't try to please everyone, serve someone specific.

🔥 Step 3: Know Your Customer

Who needs this? What do they value?

Spend time where they spend time (online or in person). **Listen before you speak.**

🔥 Step 4: Research, But Don't Drown

Study competitors. Learn pricing.

But don't get stuck in endless research. Set a timer. Learn, then move.

🔥 Step 5: Name Your Business and Secure Basics

Choose a name.

Grab the domain name and social media handles. Don't overthink. You can always refine later.

🔥 Step 6: Legal and Financial Setup

Pick your business structure (sole proprietor, LLC, etc.).

Open a separate business bank account. Keep records

from day one.

🔥 Step 7: Start Marketing Immediately

Tell people what you do.

Use free platforms (Instagram, Facebook, LinkedIn). Don't wait for perfection. **Visibility beats invisibility.**

🔥 Step 8: Set a Simple First Goal

First customer. First $100. First review. Small wins lead to big victories. **Measure progress, not perfection.**

🔥 Step 9: Build a Consistency Plan

Schedule work hours (even if small). Treat your business like a priority, not a hobby.

🔥 Step 10: Stay Connected to Your Belief

When it gets hard, return to your "why."

Pray. Reflect. Refuel. Don't let the bang push you backward.

The Bang Is Coming

The bang is coming, and that's **not** your enemy or a sign that something has gone wrong in your life.

That explosive moment is actually **proof** that something significant is happening, real movement and transformation are taking place.

Others around you might run when they hear the first signs of major change approaching their own lives. **But you'll be different.** You'll **smile with confidence** because you prepared yourself mentally and practically for this exact moment.

You stood still when others panicked. You held firmly to your beliefs when others wavered. You invested time in reading and applying the principles in this book when others chose distraction and avoidance.

You shared these insights with people who needed them and recognized that this challenging moment was actually your **breakthrough** disguised as a **test**.

Because you prepared for the bang instead of running from it, you can **embrace what's coming** with excitement rather than dread.

Money and Meaning

This preparation leads to an important understanding about **wealth** and **fulfillment** that most people never grasp.

Money itself is not evil or wrong to pursue. But **money without deeper meaning** attached to it becomes empty and ultimately unsatisfying.

Similarly, having a clear purpose is essential. But **purpose without inner peace** becomes exhausting and unsustainable over time.

The goal is to integrate both **practical success** and **spiritual fulfillment** so they support each other rather than compete for your attention and energy.

Great thinkers like **Howard Thurman** understood this principle deeply and taught that the human soul is never fulfilled by comfort alone. True satisfaction comes from meaningful contribution to something larger than your immediate needs and desires.

Viktor Frankl discovered this truth in the concentration camps. **Thurman** learned it through his work in civil rights and spiritual leadership.

Both men recognized that humans need **purpose-driven work** that serves others in order to experience **genuine fulfillment**, not just temporary pleasure.

The Right Questions

This understanding changes the questions you ask yourself about your goals and direction in life.

Instead of asking, **"What goal will make me rich?"**

Try asking, **"What goal will make me whole as a person?"**

Rather than focusing primarily on, **"How can I earn more money?"**

Consider these deeper questions:

- What would you actually do with your life if you weren't afraid of failure, rejection, or financial insecurity?
- What would you create, build, or offer to the world if you didn't fear judgment from family, friends, or society?
- What gifts, talents, or dreams have you buried or ignored in order to fit in with expectations that were never really yours to begin with?

***

These questions matter because **purpose pulls you forward** with energy and excitement toward meaningful goals, while pressure from external expectations only pushes you down into stress and resentment.

When you're operating from **authentic purpose**, challenges become **opportunities for growth**.

When you're operating from **external pressure**, the same challenges become sources of anxiety and burnout.

The difference isn't in the circumstances you face. The difference is in whether you're:

- Moving **toward** something you genuinely care about
- Or moving **away** from something you fear

How to Start Over Today

Forget the past completely, but not because it didn't matter, or because you should pretend it never happened. Your past holds valuable data: what worked, what didn't, and what you've learned through experience. But it is not your destiny, nor is it a permanent definition of who you must remain.

It happened. You survived it. You learned from it.

Now, release its hold on your future and move forward with that wisdom. Don't let yesterday's mistakes, failures, or even successes become today's limitations or excuses for staying in patterns that no longer serve your authentic growth.

You are not behind on some imaginary schedule that everyone else seems to be following successfully. You are not stuck in circumstances that can never change or improve. You are actually standing at the beginning of something completely new, with all the possibility and potential that comes with fresh starts and clear vision.

The timeline you've been measuring yourself against was created by other people's choices and circumstances. It has **nothing to do with your unique path and purpose**.

This time, as you begin again, try a completely different approach to your goals and dreams:

- Work from **alignment with your authentic values**, not external expectations.
- Stay connected to your **deeper purpose**, not just achievement checkboxes.
- **Surrender the outcome** to divine timing while remaining fully committed to right actions.

This shift in mindset changes everything, how you experience both the process and the results of your efforts.

Your Daily Fresh Start Practice

Make this simple framework your *Daily Goal Shower* for renewal and progress.

- Begin each day with **one act of focused attention** on what truly matters most to your long-term growth and fulfillment.
- Follow that with **one moment of genuine surrender**, releasing your need to control how and when your goals will be fulfilled.
- End with **one decision that actively honors your inner peace**, rather than external pressure or other people's urgent demands on your time and energy.

You don't need to figure out a comprehensive ten-year plan before you move toward positive change. You don't need to see the entire staircase before you take the first step.

What you need is the **courage and faith** to take the next faithful step in front of you, trusting that each step will reveal the next when you're ready for it.

This approach builds momentum through **consistent small actions**, rather than waiting for perfect conditions or full clarity about the distant future.

True Prosperity

Prosperity is the overflow of purpose, not the accumulation of possessions or the achievement of external status symbols meant to impress others.

True prosperity looks like this:

- **Joy that exists even when no one is watching**.
- **Rest, even when the world around you says hustle harder**.
- **Peace that refuses to be traded for the illusion of progress**.

A genuinely prosperous life is one lived in **alignment with God's timing**, not human urgency; with **God's grace**, not personal striving; with **God's peace**, not worldly anxiety about outcomes you can't control.

This kind of prosperity can't be measured by bank accounts or material wealth. It flows from **internal abundance**, a spiritual reservoir that remains steady, regardless of what's happening externally.

Stop chasing crumbs of temporary satisfaction. Stop worshipping fleeting achievements. **The table of true abundance** was already prepared for you **before you were born.**

Stop Running, Start Becoming

The time has come to stop running in frantic circles, without a clear map or destination. Stop reaching desperately for things that will never satisfy the deepest hunger of your soul.

You were not placed on this earth merely to **survive**, from paycheck to paycheck, crisis to crisis, or disappointment to disappointment.

You are here to:

- **Become the fullest expression of who God created you to be.**
- **Step into your authentic purpose.**
- **Live with permanent motivation that flows from spiritual alignment**, not external pressure.

***

Starting today, **clear your mental and spiritual atmosphere** of every voice, influence, and distraction that keeps you operating beneath your divine potential.

- Reclaim your mind from fear-based programming.
- Let go of limiting beliefs and negative thought patterns running automatically in your subconscious.
- Surrender the outcome of your efforts to divine timing and provision.

Trust this truth: Obedience to authentic spiritual

guidance will produce results that far exceed what your limited human planning could accomplish.

Choose **purpose over pressure** in every decision. Remember, sustainable success flows from alignment with your calling, not from frantic activity driven by fear.

This is your life. Live it with **intention and authenticity**.

This is your calling. Fulfill it with **courage and faith**.

This is your moment. Step into the fullness of who you were always meant to become.

You don't need permission from any human authority to pursue your authentic path. You don't need perfect conditions to begin moving toward your true destination.

What you **do** need is **presence**, spiritual and mental clarity that comes from being fully engaged with your current reality while maintaining faith in your future possibilities.

Let's move forward, into a life of **permanent motivation**, **authentic purpose**, and **divine abundance** that has been waiting for you to choose it.

Finally

If you are working a job while trying to build a business, **do not curse the very ground that is feeding your dreams**.

Some days, the job will demand all your time and strength, leaving you with nothing left for your personal vision when you get home. And on those exhausting days, when you return empty and frustrated, **don't fall into the**

trap of saying, *"I didn't accomplish anything for myself today."*

That destructive thought is a **lie**, told by impatience and misunderstanding of how success actually unfolds.

That demanding day was **already written into your story**, already factored into the **divine timeline** of your breakthrough.

You did **not** fall behind schedule. You did **not** fail your future self. You are **not** moving slower than you should be moving.

Reframing Your Current Reality

The money you earn from that job is not a detour from your real path. It is the **fuel your vision needs** to become reality.

It is:

- The wood for the fire of your dreams.
- The bridge between your current life and your future one.
- The foundation that will allow you to walk away freely when the appointed time arrives.

Be grateful for this provision. Give thanks for the stability it provides. Praise God for supplying the resources you need during this **preparation season**.

Stop hating the job, if that job is financing your freedom.

Stop despising the stepping stones that are carrying you toward your promised land.

- **Hatred** blocks the flow of blessings.
- **Bitterness** blinds you to present opportunities.
- **Resentment** builds mental barriers that slow your progress.

Gratitude sharpens your spiritual sight.

Gratitude quickens your steps toward breakthrough.

Divine Timing and Trust

Understand this fundamental truth: **The day you walk away from that job has already been scheduled on heaven's calendar**, even if you cannot see the date yet. It's already planned, already approved, and already guaranteed by divine hands that no human authority can override.

No person, economic condition, or circumstance can close a door that was built and opened by God Himself.

Faith is not just believing in the results you want to see eventually; **Faith is trusting the process**, even when the road feels endless and the rewards feel impossibly far away.

Every day you show up to that job with the right attitude, you are proving that you believe in your future. Every paycheck you receive is proof that the vision is still alive and that **provision is flowing toward your dreams**.

The Test of Gratitude

Your test during this season is not simply to endure until something better comes along. Your test is to **endure with gratitude**, to walk through heavy days with a light heart and to see beyond what is immediately in front of you, to what God is building in the unseen realm.

This requires **believing even when physical evidence of change hasn't yet arrived**.

Permanent motivation is not about constant excitement or emotional highs. It's about developing **permanent trust**:

- Trust in yourself,
- Trust in the God who created you with specific purposes,
- Trust that the seed you planted will produce fruit, even when today looks like nothing but dry dirt.

This kind of trust sustains you through ordinary days, ordinary work, and ordinary struggles, while you're building something **extraordinary**.

Your Miracle in Progress

You are not failing. You are not forgotten. You are not moving too slowly toward your goals.

You are **in the middle of your miracle**, and miracles rarely look miraculous in real time. They often appear as:

- Ordinary days,
- Ordinary work,
- Ordinary struggles,
- Ordinary people doing what needs to be done.

But hidden inside those ordinary moments is **extraordinary victory**, only visible when you look back from your breakthrough.

Hold the line with patience.

Trust the process with confidence.

Honor the work with excellence.

Give thanks for every part of the journey.

Your time is coming, with divine precision, and nothing in heaven or earth can stop what God has already set in motion.

Learning Responsibility Early

In many communities, children aren't treated like true family members with real value and purpose. Instead, they're treated more like **pets**, something to dress up, show off at gatherings, and entertain when convenient.

But **kids aren't ornaments for adult life or accessories to make parents look good**. They're integral parts of the household system and thrive when given **genuine purpose and age-appropriate responsibility**.

Children who are taught to contribute meaningfully to family life grow up with natural clarity and confidence about their place in the world. They don't wait passively to be served or entertained, they step in actively and support the family's daily functioning.

This creates a foundation of **competence and self-worth** that serves them for life.

We often talk about spouses being helpmates in marriage, but **children can also be helpmates in family life**.

I'm not suggesting giving kids inappropriate adult responsibilities. I'm talking about age-appropriate cooperation and awareness, helping them understand how their actions affect others.

When kids are treated like **valued team members**, rather

than burdens to manage or trophies to display, they develop:

- Emotional intelligence,
- Practical life skills,
- A genuine sense of belonging.

They don't just live in the home, they **belong** to it and understand their role in making it function well.

Time to Grow Up

This principle of early responsibility applies directly to your own life, **regardless of your age**.

Stop treating yourself like a child waiting for someone else to take care of everything important. **Become the adult you're capable of being right now**.

I'm not talking about legal milestones like getting a driver's license or voting. I'm talking about:

- Mental ownership of your choices,
- Emotional maturity in your relationships,
- Spiritual clarity about your purpose.

I'm speaking directly to **anyone over the age of fifteen** who still thinks adulthood can wait.

We need to stop postponing serious personal development until our thirties and forties, when life forces us to grow up. By then, many people have built what I call **"fortresses of bad habits"** and convinced themselves that these patterns are just part of their permanent personality.

They believe real adulthood begins when life hits them with consequences.

But that mindset only leads to unnecessary suffering and wasted years.

Start Now, Not Later

The problem with waiting too long is that people become **too accustomed to losing** and too good at making excuses. The wall they're trying to climb is made from their own poor choices.

They've been laying bricks of limitation since their teenage years, without realizing it. And by the time they want to change, they're dealing with **deeply rooted patterns** that require far more effort to undo.

We need to reconsider **when** people should start taking responsibility for personal development.

You don't have to wait for life to collapse around you before you start building it right. Start owning your thoughts and choices now, while you still have flexibility and energy.

Start cleaning up destructive habits **before** they become ingrained.

Start telling yourself the truth about your potential **before** the world convinces you to settle for less.

The longer you wait, the louder your excuses will become. The harder it will be to recognize your authentic self beneath layers of compromise and avoidance.

If you're reading this and feel even a spark of motivation, **act on it immediately**.

You are **not too young** to take your life seriously. And if you're older, you're **not too late** to start.

But be aware: you may be more deeply rooted in your current patterns. **Uprooting entrenched habits** takes more time and effort than planting healthy ones early on.

So, practice genuine adulthood now, **before consequences force you into it**, and you won't have to spend years recovering from choices you could've avoided.